THE PROBLEM WITH
THE HUMANISTIC THERAPIES

Other titles in the
THE PROBLEM WITH.... Series

The Problem with Cognitive Behavioural Therapy

The Problem with Psychoanalytic Psychotherapy

THE PROBLEM WITH THE HUMANISTIC THERAPIES

Nick Totton

KARNAC

First published in 2010 by
Karnac Books Ltd
118 Finchley Road
London NW3 5HT

Copyright © 2010 by Nick Totton

The right of Nick Totton to be identified as the author of this work has been asserted in accordance with §§ 77 and 78 of the Copyright Design and Patents Act 1988.

All rights reserved. No part of this publication may be reproduced, stored in a retrieval system, or transmitted, in any form or by any means, electronic, mechanical, photocopying, recording, or otherwise, without the prior written permission of the publisher.

British Library Cataloguing in Publication Data

A C.I.P. for this book is available from the British Library

ISBN-13: 978-1-85575-663-2

Typeset by Vikatan Publishing Solutions (P) Ltd., Chennai, India

Printed in Great Britain

www.karnacbooks.com

CONTENTS

PREFACE	vii
INTRODUCTION	ix
CHAPTER ONE What are the humanistic therapies?	1
CHAPTER TWO Strengths of humanistic therapies	23
CHAPTER THREE Weaknesses of humanistic therapies	41
CHAPTER FOUR How to move forward?	65
REFERENCES	81

PREFACE

There is a famous Chinese curse which runs, "May you live in interesting times". These are interesting times indeed for those who are involved in the enormous task of alleviating emotional distress. If 1 in 4 people are diagnosed at some point in their lives with a recognised form of mental illness and yet there is no magic bullet to cure this vast reservoir of human suffering, then indeed we are living in interesting times.

The threats to human life from external factors such as continuing arenas of war, global warming and feeding the world's vast population also loom. Some of these pressures precipitate illness too. Doctors and nurses working in traditional settings in mental hospitals have been augmented by a wide range of people who possess specialist knowledge in assisting people in distress. The titles of the jobs are familiar to many of us—Psychologists (of many varieties), Psychiatrists, Psychotherapists (also of many varieties), Psychoanalysts, and Counsellors and so on. The list seems endless. To a large extent all are agreed that societies in many countries have a huge problem.

When it comes to solutions, however, few professionals in the field can agree. The pressure exerted by living in interesting times means that the hunt is on to find effective cures for mental illness. The aim of *The Problem with…* series is to set out the stall for different kinds of therapies and treatments, and then demonstrate that, whatever the proposed solutions, they are not in fact a cure-all; they are accompanied by a series of potentially intractable problems.

In the short space of this preface, at least two problematic assumptions have already been made. A quick visit to the Wikipedia website informs us that the Chinese curse may, in fact, be an urban myth. A more serious question is posed by the words "mentally ill". The term itself presupposes that there is an equal and opposite condition of "mental health". Yet these terms are used to mean very different states of mind in different cultures and at other periods of time than the present.

However, the quasi-mythical Chinese curse has two faces. The experience of interesting times may be difficult—but they are indeed "interesting"! We hope that readers will be interested in these manifold problems. This is a multi-faceted, fascinating field where even the simplest definition can become mired in controversy.

The greatest problem of all that we face is the simple fact of being human. Unadulterated happiness exists only in our dreams—and often eludes us there too. In the meantime, we hope you enjoy reading this series.

Kirsty Hall
Series Editor

INTRODUCTION

> There has been much hand-wringing over everything having to do with the label 'humanistic,' including proposals to even abandon the name. Its body has been declared headless without a new generation of visionary leaders; its head has been declared heartless because it has conformed so much to the mainstream that it no longer acts on its prerogative for incisive dissent, and its heart has been declared brainless for being still too anti-intellectual. Meanwhile, others have declared that the whole humanistic organism has been dead for decades because its votaries have never moved out of the 1960s.
>
> (Eugene Taylor, 1999, p. 11)

My original psychotherapy training was as a Reichian body psychotherapist. It was a thoroughly humanistic style of training; but when I later wrote an MA dissertation on Reich, I realised that although several humanistic modalities were initiated by ex-psychoanalysts, Reich was the only one of these who never himself renounced analysis (but was thrown out, in a complex piece of politicking partly aimed at appeasing the

Nazis (Jacoby, 1986, pp. 91–3). In fact, Reichian ideas make a lot more sense if they are understood as a development, or in some ways a restatement, of psychoanalysis.

This interesting mix—psychoanalytic content in a humanistic style—has in many ways defined my work as a therapist, and sums up my credentials for writing this book. Throughout my career I have learnt from both approaches: after my Reichian training, the two biggest inputs into my work were an MA in Psychoanalytic Studies, and a number of long and short workshops in Process Oriented Psychology. I have always found friends and peers in both psychodynamic and humanistic circles, and have attracted trainees and clients from both fields; several trainees have told me that the work I teach seems to them very similar to person-centred therapy, several others that it reminds them of Gestalt, and still others that it is essentially psychodynamic.

However I am not a practitioner of any modality of humanistic therapy, nor am I trained in any (though I have been a client of humanistic practitioners). This gives me certain advantages as an impartial observer; but it also means that what I have to say about the humanistic therapies is from an outsider's viewpoint, and based ultimately as much on what I have read and heard as on what I have experienced. I am certain that there are things in this book, which insiders will see as ill-informed or as misunderstandings. I would ask them to consider that these will be the mistakes of an experienced and sympathetic observer, and that they may therefore represent problems of communication for humanistic therapy.

One major problem for humanistic therapy is not of its own making: as a later arrival on the scene than psychoanalytic therapy, it is inevitably defined and described in contrast to it rather than in its own right. This is perhaps why its own self-descriptions tend strongly to be insular, and often ignorant of what other people are up to. The standard depiction of psychoanalytic work by humanistic writers is around

50 years out of date. But of course much the same is true the other way around; and the analytic world's tendency to ignore the very existence of humanistic work is infuriating in the extreme. It reminds me of the joke about a new arrival being shown around the afterlife, visiting the Jewish heaven, the Muslim heaven, and so on, until she approaches a high wall with the sound of singing coming from inside. 'Sssshh,' whispers her guide, 'that's the Christian heaven, they don't think anyone else is here.'

There are many private heavens in the therapy world; and if this book contributes to demolishing a few walls, I shall be very pleased.

The book is structured according to the series blueprint. Chapter One tries to describe in outline what the humanistic therapies are, both in general terms and characterising each of the 'big three', Gestalt therapy, Rogerian therapy or counselling, and Transactional Analysis. Chapter Two looks at the strengths of humanistic work, while Chapter Three turns each of these around and examines its weaknesses. Chapter Four then looks at possible futures for humanistic work in a fairly inhospitable environment.

I would like to thank Kirsty Hall for inviting me to write this book, and for her support in the process of doing so; Pete Sanders, for some help with references; Professor Mick Cooper, for helping me avoid an egregious error; and all of my humanistically-oriented friends, colleagues and trainees, past and present, for their indefinable but considerable contribution.

CHAPTER ONE

What are the humanistic therapies?

When we speak of 'the humanistic therapies' or 'humanistic therapy', we are referring to a group of approaches which appeared in the USA in the 1940s and 1950s, becoming more defined at the Old Saybrook Conference of 1964 (Bugental, 1965) where many of the best-known figures came together under the banner of 'Humanistic Psychology'. 'Therapy' and 'psychology' are intertwined, and sometimes used interchangeably—especially in the United States where many therapists refer to themselves as psychologists—but strictly speaking, humanistic psychology is the academic study, and humanistic therapy the clinical practice. (For authoritative surveys of the field, see Cain, 2001; Schneider, Bugental and Pierson, 2001.)

The three big beasts of humanistic therapy are Gestalt; Transactional Analysis; and Person-Centred, Client-Centred or Rogerian work (which often describes itself as counselling rather than psychotherapy). Flourishing among these big three is an entire ecosystem of smaller therapies, some of them independent approaches, others blends or integrations of elements from the big three with or without the addition of psychodynamic thinking and/or various of the smaller humanistic therapies. Significant elements are the range of body-based approaches, including Reichian and neo-Reichian therapies, and the expressive therapies centred on art, drama and movement.

There have also always been a number of practitioners who, rather than belonging to or starting a school, identify themselves simply as 'humanistic therapists'. Well-known examples are John Rowan in the UK, and Abraham Maslow and Will Schutz in the USA. And although less common than previously, there are still trainings available in the UK and the USA which offer a qualification not in a specific humanistic modality but generally in humanistic, or 'humanistic and integrative', therapy; the latter phrase matching the name of the relevant section of the UK Council for Psychotherapy (UKCP).

Everything in the previous paragraphs will be unpacked in what follows; what is important straight away is to realise the range and variety of humanistic therapies, the number of distinct, often contrasting and sometimes conflicting approaches which are included under that title. So what, if anything, do the humanistic therapies have in common? What makes them all 'humanistic'?

The name itself is in fact the first problem we encounter. 'Humanistic' in this context has a highly idiosyncratic meaning, distinct from the usual use of the word to indicate a non-religious ethical position. 'Humanistic therapy' derives from 'humanistic psychology', a term which originally flagged up a concern about *de*humanization, and a celebration of 'human potential' (another term often used for these therapies) against the perceived machine values of modern society. The approach was also claimed to be more *humane*, more warm-blooded and relational, than its two colleagues or rivals, the psychodynamic and behaviourist traditions.

It is apparent from this that 'humanistic' has no very clearly defined meaning, but more of an impressionistic effect. Other labels covering some of the same ground are 'the growth movement', 'the human potential movement', and 'the third wave' (after psychoanalysis and behaviourism). There is a notably political flavour to this talk of movements and waves; and many humanistic pioneers did indeed see themselves as forming a revolutionary movement, which wanted to overturn the orthodoxies of the past. Alternatively, movements and waves could be seen as cultural or artistic, and again there is a strong link between humanistic therapy and creative expression.

Because of this impressionistic effect, though, and because humanistic therapy is essentially a loose alliance of independent schools, which arose separately within similar milieus, it is not easy to establish a shared creed. John Rowan (1998), a veteran of the humanistic scene, identifies three key positions, which he believes are common to all humanistic approaches: self-actualization, integration, and growth. The first and third of these seem to me inseparable, and I am treating them together as 'the actualizing tendency', substituting Rogers' better-known terminology for Maslow's (1968) to avoid confusion, since Rogerians use 'self-actualization' in a different sense (Sanders, 2006, 30–32). However, I intend the term to apply to similar formulations in other humanistic systems. I am also adding what seems to me another key position, egalitarianism, between actualizing and integration. I will look at each of these in turn, noting some contrasts with psychodynamic approaches, and also some problems with or questions about humanistic therapy's positions.

The actualizing tendency

This ungainly term refers to what Carl Rogers calls 'a directional tendency inherent in the human organism—a tendency to grow, to develop, to realize its full potential' (Rogers, 1986, p. 127). The emphasis is less on *reaching* one's full potential, than on tending *towards* it; new possibilities always open up in the direction of growth. Belief in actualizing is inseparable from a positive view of human nature, a belief that at the most fundamental level (some would say, at the point of birth) human beings are good and creative. In TA terms, we are all basically 'OK' (Harris, 1967); or as Wilhelm Reich puts it, 'under favourable conditions, man is an essentially honest, industrious, cooperative, loving, and, if motivated, rationally hating animal' (Reich, 1975 [1946], p. 13). Therapy, therefore, seeks to uncover this fundamental OKness, or to help it reveal itself. Humanistic therapists hold that there is an inherent tendency to actualize in every one of us, and therefore focus on supporting what in their view is already trying to happen.

This approach can entail a startlingly optimistic therapeutic programme, which as we shall see came together in the 1960s and 1970s with a political optimism about social change. Eric Berne, founder of Transactional Analysis, said in 1966 'We don't want patients to make progress ... We want them to get well. Or, in our lingo, we want to turn frogs into princes. We're not satisfied with making them braver frogs' (Languth, 1966). This contrasts strongly with the more modest aims of most psychodynamic approaches, especially Kleinian ones, which emphasize the negative emotions we all experience and see as our best option the compromise of 'the depressive position' (Klein, 1998). Freud himself famously claimed only to turn 'hysterical misery into common unhappiness' (Freud and Breuer, 1955 [1893–5], p. 305).

It also contrasts with the 'medical model' of therapy, which, after a period of relative eclipse, has now returned to dominance. This model draws a dubious analogy between psychological unhappiness and physical disease, and tasks therapy with reducing or eliminating symptoms—that is, difficult feelings and behaviour—without necessarily considering their cause. The medical model has always been present in therapy; most of the first practitioners were doctors. Its current return has a lot to do with the need to find ways of funding therapy, which led practitioners into the NHS or insurance-based work, and also into voluntary organisations providing free or low cost therapy. So that they know they are getting something for their money, funders reasonably demand an 'evidence-based approach' of symptom relief, which is however fundamentally incompatible with the humanistic emphasis on growth and actualization. Pursuit of the latter may well lead to the former, but often by indirect routes, and occasionally not at all, while pursuit of the former may have little or no connection with the latter, or even—in the case of some chemical treatments, for example—be inimical to it.

The obvious query about this humanistic tenet is: If we are fundamentally good and actualizing, why do we need therapy at all? How does it come about that people don't feel or act as if they are OK? The answer generally given, in one form or another (e.g., Rogers, 1961, Perls, Hefferline and Goodman, 1973, Reich, 1975), is that the values and structures of Western society, as mediated through the family, tend to suppress our OKness. As Eric Berne again puts it, 'People are born princes and princesses, until their parents turn them into frogs' (Steiner, 1990, p. 2; often quoted in a watered-down and sexist form as 'We're born princes and the civilizing process turns us into frogs.') This answer, in many ways a strong one, does create a further and quite difficult question: If we are all inherently positive beings, how did such a negative family and social system first come into being?

Similar queries can be raised around humanistic therapy's belief in the inherent tendency of human beings to *develop* positively. The difficulty here is that we have evidence all around us of people's *failure* to grow, in this sense of creative unfolding. It is generally acknowledged by humanistic therapists that the impulse to growth is fragile, and easily overwhelmed or even eliminated by adverse conditions (Sheldon and Kasser, 2001). As with actualizing, the question then arises: Where do these adverse conditions originate?

Egalitarianism

As a corollary of their belief in the actualizing tendency, the humanistic therapies take an egalitarian attitude towards their clients. This is shown straight away in the choice of the term 'client' to described those who use therapy; traditionally both psychoanalysis and psychiatry of course use 'patient', placing the work firmly within a medical model (analysts sometimes use the more open term 'analysand'). A *patient* is by definition sick, 'suffering' (the word's etymological root), in a position of deficit. *Client* is borrowed from commercial transactions, and intended to indicate a fair exchange between peers of money for services (though it unfortunately also has a more dependent connotation, as in 'client state'); indeed, some humanistic practitioners draw up a therapeutic contract outlining the expectations and responsibilities of each party (Stewart and Joines, 1987, pp. 260–5).

The deeper implication is that the client can be relied on to function as an adult, no matter how deeply the work connects them with more infantile feelings. Richard Mowbray has coined the acronym SAFAA to describe this assumption— 'Sufficient Available Functioning Adult Autonomy' (Mowbray, 1995, p. 183). The TA therapist Carl Steiner writes:

> People in emotional difficulties are nevertheless full, intelligent human beings. They are capable of understanding their troubles and the process which liberates people from them. They must be involved in the healing process if they are to solve their difficulties.
> (Steiner, 1990, p. 1)

This is a very significant affirmation of basic equality in the therapeutic work. The potential difficulties are many, however, and we will be returning to them. Some would argue that many clients are in fact *not* capable of understanding their troubles or acting in an adult way, at least not all the time; and it is potentially abusive to treat a client as a functioning adult when they are not. Mowbray acknowledges that the SAFAA approach is not suitable for everyone (1995, p. 184). Some therapies, particularly psychodynamic ones, think that that clients often need to move into a *less* rational and autonomous position during therapy (Van Sweden, 1995).

Integration

The humanistic therapies have a strong tendency towards *wholism*—that is, treating human beings as united body, mind and spirit, each essential to the whole but none able to stand on its own. More contemporary metaphors might be a hologram, where all the information is contained in each part; or fractals, where the same pattern is repeated on every level of detail. Hence humanistic therapies seek to encourage and support the integration of these facets of our being, and to point out how we tend, damagingly, to split ourselves and even to devalue particular facets—a process, which is widely seen as socially conditioned.

Wholism is of course sometimes little more than a pious incantation, and either 'united body, mind and spirit' means something to you, or it doesn't; there is nothing here that can be proved or disproved (though on the inseparability of body and mind, see Totton, 1998). It is also true that many humanistic therapists tend in practice to privilege bodily experience and emotions over intellectual processes. This can be justified as a rebalancing of a general cultural tendency in the reverse direction; but it is still not exactly wholistic. However, there is certainly a strong value placed in humanistic work on the integration of different aspects of ourselves. Rowan identifies five such aspects:

> If we say that human beings exist on at least five levels—body, feelings, intellect, soul and spirit—then we have to do justice to all five of these levels in all our efforts at realising human potential. If I want to be that self which I truly am, then I have to be it on all five of these levels.
> (Rowan, 1998, p. 3; cf Schutz, 1979, p. 17)

Varieties of humanistic therapy

Having indicated some unifying factors in the humanistic therapies, I will now distinguish between the main approaches; describing identifying features of the 'big three'—Rogerian, Gestalt and Transactional Analysis—and also of body oriented and expressive therapies. Necessarily, these outlines are simplified, and almost every assertion could be qualified or nuanced in several ways; also, none of these modalities are monolithic, and some practitioners will always see things differently.

Rogerian therapy

> Currently, in Britain … the largest therapeutic discipline is person-centered therapy. In Britain, there are more training places filled on person-centered courses than those based on other models. Also, person-centered book sales are marginally ahead of psychodynamic and several times as large as behavioral, cognitive behavioral, and rational emotive behavioral therapy combined.
>
> (Mearns, 2003, p. 55)

As already mentioned, Rogerian work—inspired, that is, by Carl Rogers—most often refers to itself as 'counselling' rather than psychotherapy. This is famously because Rogers himself, a clinical psychologist by training, was unable to practise as a psychotherapist. But more importantly, the new term was coined as an egalitarian alternative to what Rogers saw as the rather grandiose pretensions of psychotherapy and psychiatry—indicating the offer of *help* rather than *treatment*.

Rogerian work is also widely known as 'person-centred' or 'client-centred', these labels being intended to indicate the specific nature of the help being offered. (I am using the term 'Rogerian' to avoid siding with one or other of these two terms, which are to some degree in competition.) Rogerians do not see themselves as offering their clients solutions, but as helping the client to find their own solutions, following their own path. They seek to do this by providing a context in which people's creative intelligence can flourish; and according to Rogers (1957, 1959), this context is constructed from three key elements, empathy, congruence, and unconditional positive regard. (Rogers actually identified six 'conditions for therapeutic change', but many—though not all—Rogerians emphasise these three [Sanders, 2006, pp. 7–8].)

Rogers believed that these three 'core conditions', manifested by the practitioner, are both necessary and sufficient to activate the 'actualizing tendency' which is the engine for positive change and problem-solving. The meaning of *empathy* is well-known: the ability to feel with another person, to grasp their experience and in particular their emotional pain, while still remaining firmly anchored in one's own subjectivity. *Congruence* is also often referred to as genuineness or authenticity: the practitioner needs to be a convincingly real person, rather than simply manifesting a role. And *unconditional positive regard* means the capacity to accept and welcome whatever the client expresses, without judgement or expectation, while holding a steady belief in the client's ability to change and grow.

Bozarth (1998) argues convincingly that this third core condition is the crucial one; with empathy and congruence helping to enable the client to trust that the practitioner's unconditional positive regard is real and reliable. Over the last half-century several people have suggested revisions or extensions of the core conditions, primarily along the lines that, while *necessary* for therapeutic change, these conditions may not be *sufficient*, so that other additional techniques may be required (Carkhuff, 1969; Gelso and Carter, 1985). Probably the great majority of Rogerians, however, cleave to the three core conditions, with the necessary implication that most of the required training will be focused on the trainees' work on themselves so that they can become able to manifest these qualities (Mearns, 2003, p. 57).

Given this focus, a great deal of the very extensive Rogerian literature is devoted to exploring the core conditions: unpacking their implications, discussing how they apply in different situations, finding parallels in other traditions and philosophies, considering how people might be taught or helped to manifest them, exploring clinical cruxes and dilemmas in terms of the core conditions, and so on. One of the ongoing controversies is about whether the core conditions are best thought of as *aspirations*, states which one might occasionally achieve while mostly falling short to a greater or lesser extent; or as *foundations*, states which should form a reliable ground on which every practitioner stands. There are eminent Rogerians who argue each position (Litaer, 1984; Bozarth, 1998). The core conditions militate against the use of any form of technique, though to the outside eye techniques do appear to exist—for example, the extensive use of paraphrase, offering back to the client a reworded version of what they have just told the therapist.

Gestalt therapy

Like several humanistic approaches, Gestalt originated in the work of a disaffected psychoanalyst, Fritz Perls (though recently more emphasis has been placed on the importance of other early gestaltists, notably Fritz's wife Laura Perls and his student Isadore From). It is from Gestalt that the humanistic therapies take one of their most widely used slogans, 'Be in the here and now' (cf. Perls, Hefferline and Goodman, 1973, pp. 59). Gestalt seeks to enable a spontaneous, contactful, responsive attitude to life, uninhibited by internalised commands or taboos or by rigid defensive strategies.

The originators of Gestalt drew upon Gestalt psychology for their theoretical base, also borrowing the name. Gestalt psychology (Goldstein, 1995 [1934]) considers human perception and action to be a series of meaningful organisations of sense data (in German 'gestalt' means 'form or shape') and responses to this organisation. Human beings make meaning out of their environment, always and already an *active* perception: we pull out part of the perceptual field as 'figure', and allow the rest to sink back as 'ground'. What is figure and what is ground is a matter of what is most interesting to a particular person at a particular moment: for someone dying of thirst, the glass of water in the bottom left corner will become the immediate centre of attention. Perls himself used taking in nourishment as his most consistent model of the relation between organism and environment (Perls, 1969a); and metaphors of tasting, biting, chewing, swallowing, digesting, and pushing out permeate Gestalt theory.

Gestalt therapy regards the lively, fluid creation, completion and replacement of gestalts as the natural human state; and therefore pays attention to processes which take us out of contact with what is immediately present—what are called 'contact boundary disturbances' (Latner, 1992). Whatever patterns are recognised in people's process, there is a continuous effort to avoid creating the sorts of hypostatised entities ('the unconscious', 'character structure', 'ego states') which are so common in many forms of therapy, and to stick with the concrete and immediate. The practice of Gestalt therapy is centred on bringing the client back into contact with their here-and-now experience, using judo-like techniques to interrupt their avoidance patterns. Gestaltists invite their clients to enter into practical explorations of their own process: 'Gestalt therapy brings self-realization through here-and-now experiments in directed awareness' (Yontef, 1975, p. 34).

Many of these experiments focus on bodily experience; Barry Stevens (1977, p. 160) characterises this as 'learning how to decontrol my body'. We can get a flavour of the Gestalt attitude from Stevens' suggestions to a client experiencing bodily pain or tension:

> See if you can explore it—gently, not pushing it around, like getting friendly with it—and see if you can discover

what wants to happen there and let it happen. See if some movement grows out of the pain or tension. It may be some very small movement that you can be aware of that is not visible to me. It may be a large movement that I can see. Let it do whatever it wants to do.

(Stevens, 1977, p. 162)

The style of Gestalt therapy varies enormously between practitioners, with some working in a confrontational and even abrasive way (following the tradition of Fritz Perls himself), and others working much more gently and relationally. Several different emphases have of course developed over the last half-century. Classical Gestalt focuses on exploring local experience through a series of 'experiments' with one's perceptions, awareness and impulses—for example:

Try for a few minutes to make up sentences stating what you are at this moment aware of. Begin each sentence with the words 'now' or 'at this moment' or 'here and now'.
(Perls, Hefferline and Goodman, 1971, p. 59)

This and the other experiments are of course intended for the reader/client; but working as a therapist requires a similar state of being.

Alongside this sort of *intra*personal emphasis, there was always an intense awareness of the importance of the *inter*personal aspects of contact; and Gestalt as a 'two body therapy' was developed more strongly in the 60s and 70s (Polster and Polster, 1974). Currently, there is a tendency to stress the importance of field theory (Parlett, 1997, 2005), based on the inseparability of figure and ground, organism and environment, so that 'the "somebody" that I am being is a field event' (Philippson, 2002). Each of these elements was already present in Gestalt's initial formulations; but different schools and theorists focus on different themes.

Transactional Analysis

While Gestalt tries to avoid structures and systems wherever possible, Transactional Analysis (TA) finds them very useful, and indeed almost specialises in creating punchy and memorable systematisations, starting out from Eric Berne's famous description of the three 'ego-states' of Parent, Adult and Child (Berne, 1968, pp. 23; cf. Stewart and Joines, 1987, pp. 11). Like Perls, Berne trained originally as a psychoanalyst; and the Parent/Adult/Child system (PAC) is in a sense—though only in a sense—a version of Freud's superego, ego and id.

However, typically of the TA approach, PAC is very much an operational tool rather than a metapsychological entity. Berne defined an ego-state as 'a system of feelings accompanied by a related set of behaviour patterns' (Berne 1968, p. 23; he refers to 'ego states', but the contemporary usage is hyphenated); and TA is not hugely interested in the existential status of ego-states, or in concepts like the unconscious, but rather in the usefulness of learning to recognise different ego-states in oneself and in others.

> When I am behaving, thinking and feeling as I did when I was a child, I am said to be in my *Child ego-state*.
>
> When I am behaving, thinking and feeling in ways I copied from parents or parent-figures, I am said to be in my *Parent ego-state*.
>
> When I am behaving, thinking and feeling in ways which are a direct here-and-now response to events around me, using all the abilities I have as a grown-up, I am said to be in my *Adult ego-state*.
> (Stewart and Joines, 1987, p. 11)

There are several difficulties one might raise here, but I will reserve them for Chapter Three. A major part of the TA therapist's job is to educate the client in recognising their own shifts between ego-states, and the advantages and drawbacks of each state in different situations. TA has also extensively explored what it calls 'crossed transactions', the interpersonal difficulties which arise when people are communicating from different ego-states, for example Parent to Child and vice versa (Berne, 1968, pp. 28–32; Stewart and Joines, 1987, pp. 62–5).

TA has coined a number of other interesting and useful concepts, perhaps most notably the 'life script'.

> Script theory is based on the belief that people make conscious life plans in childhood or early adolescence which influence and make predictable the rest of their lives. Persons whose lives are based on such decisions are said to have scripts.
>
> (Steiner, 1990, p. 23)

Generally a life script is based on inadequate or out-dated information, and the more rigidly it is followed, the less good the results are likely to be. Situations like suicide, drug addiction or psychosis all result from scripts, and hence, in TA's view, are all capable of being changed.

Like 'script', many TA terms have become part of the common currency of humanistic therapies, often without much grasp of their precise technical meaning. Other examples include 'strokes' (defined as 'units of recognition'—all the ways in which people acknowledge each other's existence, verbally and non-verbally); the 'rescue triangle' or 'drama triangle' (Steiner, 1990, pp. 146–54, 235–42); and, of course, the famous 'game'. A game in TA is 'a recurring set of transactions, often repetitious, superficially plausible, with a concealed motivation; or, more colloquially, a series of moves with a snare, or "gimmick"' (Berne, 1968, p. 44). The games that a person chooses to play derive from their life script. Berne (1968) and other TA theorists have identified many different games, often with self-explanatory names like 'Why Don't You—Yes But', 'Let's You and Him Fight' and 'See What You Made Me Do'.

It is apparent from this outline that TA is inventive, imaginative, observant, eloquent and fun. Many of its formulations are instantly recognisable and clearly relevant to the sorts of difficulties which bring people to therapy. What is less apparent—and this may or may not be seen as important—is how far TA theory is a valid set of general theorems, and how far it consists of a series of spectacular improvisations.

Body centred therapies

The first body centred therapy was Wilhelm Reich's orgonomy, developed to its furthest point in the USA in the 1950s. Although Reich was a psychoanalyst who, unlike Eric Berne or Fritz Perls, never actually renounced his roots, Reichian therapy was largely assimilated to the humanistic world after Reich was expelled from the International Psychoanalytic Association and finally settled in the US after World War II (Sharaf, 1983, 186ff, 262ff). Reich continued to get in trouble in America as he had with the analysts and with the authorities in Nazi Germany and Scandinavia; he died in prison in 1956, having been gaoled for contempt of court after he was forbidden to continue his work with subtle energy devices (Sharaf, 1983, pp. 446).

Although orthodox Reichian orgonomy continues to be practiced, Reich's work has also given birth to a number of more widely known neo- or post-Reichian schools, most of them functioning within a more or less humanistic framework of ideas and techniques. Alexander Lowen's Bioenergetics (Lowen, 1994) is a partial exception, in that it draws strongly on analytic concepts; but simply working with the body, and in particular with touch, is enough to exclude any therapy from participating in the analytic communion (although this is beginning to change; see for example Anderson, 2008). Dance Movement Therapy (DMT) is a distinct set of approaches to working with the body, which includes both psychoanalytic and humanistic methodologies of various different kinds (Bernstein, 1979).

There are now a number of approaches to body psychotherapy (often under the rubric of 'somatic therapy') with roots in traditions other than Reichian work, all of them generally speaking part of the humanistic world. As we have seen, Gestalt therapy has a strong bodily focus; like all true body *psychotherapies*, it integrates this into a wholistic approach which utilises verbal as well as physical techniques, and psychological as well as somatic models. Other body psychotherapy modalities, some more and some less aligned with humanistic therapy, are described in Totton (2003).

Expressive arts therapies

Another tribe of humanistic therapies are those which use one form or another of art as their central tool. DMT overlaps with this category; other members are humanistic forms of art therapy proper, utilising painting, drawing, clay and so on (Dalley and Case, 2006); those who work with voice and with music (Bunt and Hoskyns, 2002); and some forms of dramatherapy, psychodrama and so on (Jones, 2007; Karp et al., 1998). Again, some versions of each of these are humanistic, others are not. Some, like the person-centred expressive therapy of Carl Rogers's daughter Natalie Rogers (1993), are direct descendants of a specific humanistic school.

Blends, integrations and in-betweeners

In keeping with the tendency to spontaneity of humanistic therapy, there are many groups or individual practitioners working with a combination of some or all of the above approaches, often also including a psychodynamic input and sometimes a cognitive behavioural one. When there has been an attempt to order and synthesise these various elements, the approach is generally termed 'integrative'; when therapy is seen more as a matter of choosing the best tool for a particular situation, the approach is often called 'eclectic' (Norcross, 2005; Lazarus, 2005). The psychoanalyst Christopher Bollas argues eloquently for the value of an eclectic approach, which he terms 'pluralistic':

> If one has more ways of seeing mental life and human behaviour then, in my view, it follows logically that one is going to be more effective ... If your preconscious stores multiple models of the mind and behaviour, to be activated by work with a particular patient in a particular moment, then you will find that you are either consciously or unconsciously envisioning the patient through one or another of these lenses.
>
> (Bollas, 2007, p. 7)

Perhaps as a corollary of the clinical tendency to integration discussed earlier, humanistic therapies seem drawn to integration at the level of theory and practice. The relevant section of the UK Council for Psychotherapy (UKCP) is in fact called the Humanistic and Integrative Section, and includes several training bodies which teach an integrative approach, for example the Bath Centre for Psychotherapy and Counselling and the Minster Centre. There are also many individual practitioners—mostly of an older generation—ploughing their own furrow and using whatever blend of approaches feels right to them; a distinguished example is John Rowan (1998).

Political and spiritual dimensions

Right across the range of the humanistic therapies, there has historically been a strong radical political trend. In the 1960s and 1970s, humanistic therapy and radical politics synchronised and synergised with each other, producing groups like the Berkeley Radical Psychiatry Centre and the Chicago-based Changes group in the USA (Totton, 2000, pp. 25–9, 68–9). Many central humanistic figures produced writings during this period which strongly supported the radical movements in society. Carl Rogers published *Carl Rogers on Personal Power: Inner Strength and Its Revolutionary Impact* (1978), arguing that the core conditions were intrinsically 'a challenging political statement' (1978, p. 9). Erving and Miriam Polster (1974) took a similar position about Gestalt, relating it to the 'loosening up of poisonous taboos' in society (ibid, p. 26); and of course Perls, Hefferline and Goodman (1973, e.g., pp. 400–1) had already made powerful statements of opposition to conventional values in the 1950s. As for Transactional Analysis, Carl Steiner, a leading figure in its development, was a key member of the Berkeley political scene working on the journal *Issues In Radical Therapy* (Wyckoff, 1976), and later published the classic *The Other Side of Power* (Steiner, 1981).

With the ebbing of the radical tide in the 1980s and subsequently, however, humanistic therapy entered the conventional mainstream, at least relative to its earlier positions. Like ex-radicals in every walk of life, veteran therapists tend either to dislike being reminded of their earlier beliefs, or to treat them as relics of a colourful youth. There are of course many honourable exceptions: Carl Steiner, for example, continues to fight his corner; and there is a younger generation of Rogerians, in particular, who have taken up the political implications of humanistic therapy (Procter, Cooper and Sanders, 2006).

In a parallel way, and also stemming from its close connection with the hippy counter-culture of the 1960s and 1970s, humanistic therapy has always been friendly to spiritual and transpersonal experiences and ways of understanding; Rowan suggests that 'a client is a spiritual being on a spiritual path (even though they may not be aware of it yet' (1998, p. 45). We shall look further at this aspect in the next two chapters.

Groups

There has always been a strong emphasis in humanistic therapies on the use of experiential groups (Berne, 1966; Perls, 1971; Rogers, 1973; Whitton, 2003, pp. 19–24; Page and Berkow, 2005). Carl Rogers was the originator of the encounter group model, and both TA and Gestalt have traditionally done a lot of work in groups rather than one to one, and continue to do so. Of course other modalities also use groups, but for psychodynamic therapists they tend to be seen as a specialism requiring separate training; while in humanistic circles someone trained as a practitioner will have spent a good deal of time in groups during their training, and will often be regarded as inherently competent to lead them.

Sometimes humanistic groups are structured mainly around the facilitator's work with individual members, while the rest of the group acts mainly as a witnessing audience. However there is usually at least an element of interaction between group members, ranging all the way to the encounter group structure where group interaction is the central process involved. In its pure form, an encounter group is a space where 'there is no structure … except what we provide. We do not know our purposes, we do not even know each other, and we are committed to remain together over a considerable period of time' (Rogers, 1973, p. 22). As Rogers comments (ibid), 'in this situation, confusion and frustration are natural'; what he found, however, and what many subsequent facilitators have confirmed, is that the situation stimulates a *collective* actualization process, which supports not only individual growth, but also the resolution of many organisational and institutional difficulties.

Conclusion: The humanistic atmosphere

There is something crucial missing from the above account: what we might call the atmosphere or tone of the humanistic therapies—both their shared tone, and the very significant differences between them. Compared to psychodynamic approaches (and there are of course many possible qualifications and nuances to all this), humanistic therapy brings a marked sense of *activity*, of something being *done* (cf. Rowan, 1998, pp. 10–11). Humanistic practitioners tend to come out to meet their clients, visibly reacting and responding to them and their stories, rolling up their sleeves and engaging with them in a 'What needs sorting out here?' style. While the difference from psychodynamic work is around activity, the difference from CBT approaches is around *responsiveness*, being moved and stirred by the client's humanity.

Of the therapies described above, Rogerian work conforms least to the 'activity' model. Rogerians resist the demand that something be done by the therapist, and try instead to engage the client's own power to change through offering them unconditional positive regard. However, compared with much psychodynamic work there is still a greater sense of the therapist's active presence, deriving from the emphasis on congruence: for unconditional positive regard to be effective, it has to come from a person whom the client perceives to be real and authentic, warts and all.

'Warts and all' might almost be a rallying cry of the humanistic movement. John Rowan suggests that the therapist should base their choice of responses on the idea that 'Whatever is thoroughly genuine and personally felt is probably going to be all right' (Rowan, 1998, p. 36). This sort of attitude necessarily implies at least sometimes letting one's imperfections, bad moods, prejudices, confusions and failures be visible to the client. 'Self-disclosure' is not a bad word in humanistic circles.

So there is a shared 'felt sense' in humanistic work which can be approximated through the following splatter of words: 'spontaneous—vital—energetic—contactful—present—improvising—active—embodied—personal—concrete—open—sensuous'. This is not to say that any of these words might not be used of or by particular practitioners in other traditions; but the set of words that one would choose to characterise the psychodynamic atmosphere, for example, would certainly be rather different.

As I have already suggested, within this overall tone there are significant distinctions between the atmospheres of different humanistic therapies: Gestalt, we might fairly say, is the most active, Rogerian the most tending to follow the client, TA the most structured. And individual practitioners will always vary, often to a greater degree *within* orientations than *between* them. Given all this, though, I think that the overall felt sense of humanistic therapy is a real phenomenon, and perhaps the most important thing to keep a grip on in what follows.

CHAPTER TWO

Strengths of humanistic therapies

In this chapter I will list and examine ten features of humanistic therapy which seem to me creative and valuable. I have a few reservations about some of these, but will endeavour to present them here in the best possible light (and I do genuinely believe that they are all valuable). In the next chapter, I will look at ten corresponding weaknesses—that is, at the shadow side, as humanistic therapists might term it, of these same ten distinguishing features. Cast as strengths, these features are:

- A positive view of human nature
- A focus on growth, not cure
- Empowering to clients
- A style which is closer to ordinary communicating
- A contactful way of relating
- Spontaneous and improvising
- A positive attitude to embodiment and emotions
- A positive attitude to spirituality
- An inherent social critique
- An experiential paradigm of practice and research.

1 Positive view of human nature

As already indicated in Chapter One, humanistic therapy is founded on an optimistic perception of human beings and their potential, which in the therapy room translates into an optimistic perception of the client and their life decisions. 'All clients have within themselves vast resources for development. They have the capacity to grow towards the fulfilment of their unique identities, which means that self-concepts are not unalterable and attitudes or behaviours can be modified or transformed' (Mearns and Thorne, 1999, p. 14).

The basic assumption, repeated by many writers in many different ways, is that each individual has made the best choices available to her given the particular circumstances of her life, and hence deserves affirmation and support rather than criticism; and further, that 'within a favourable context, including therapy, people can discover new ways of thinking and acting' (Whitton, 2003, p. 41)—ways which will be more creative and more pleasant than the familiar ones.

One of the practical goals of therapy is therefore to transmit this view to the client, to enable her to internalise it and thus to gentle the internal critical voices which make change so hard for us, and constitute one of our greatest burdens. The 'internal critic' or 'inner critic' is a feature of many humanistic approaches and self-help books (Bradshaw, 1988; Stone and Stone, 1993), and is by no means interchangeable with the Freudian 'superego'. Hal and Sidra Stone describe it like this:

> The Inner Critic ... is that inner voice that criticizes us and speaks about us in a disparaging way. It makes everything look ugly. Most of us are not even aware that it is a voice or self speaking inside us because its constant judgements have been with us since early childhood and its running critical commentary feels like a natural part of ourselves. It develops early in our lives, absorbing the judgements of the people around us and the expectations of the society

in which we live .... As long as we are unconscious of it, we must constantly appease it.

(Stone and Stone, 1993, pp. 4–5)

Identifying and conceptualising this aspect of the psyche has been a valuable contribution of humanistic therapy, especially when accompanied by effective techniques for freeing oneself from the power of the inner critic and utilising its capacity to assess and evaluate in more constructive ways (see Stone and Stone, 1993). From this point of view one could argue that psychodynamic and existential therapies have been over-influenced by this inner critical voice in their pessimistic emphasis on flawedness, fallibility and destructiveness.

In my view the strength of the positive emphasis in humanistic work is not in any concrete assertion it makes about how people function—and certainly not in New Age mantras about everything being for the best (see Chapter Three)—but in a fundamental groundedness in the world and in our own embodiment, a felt sense that *here and now is all right*, which can be communicated from therapist to client with transformative effect.

2   Growth not cure

Because humanistic therapists take a basically positive view of human beings, they tend not to emphasise their faults and problems in the same style that some other practitioners might; in particular, there is little emphasis on what one might call structural problems, or 'psychopathology'. Instead, there is a focus on the potential for 'growth', an ongoing process of becoming-more-oneself not dissimilar to Jung's 'individuation' (Clark, 2006), and which, like Jung, humanistic therapists see as an inherent tendency which will be activated in each individual in the right circumstances . It has been suggested that 'this *positive* growth-based assumption may be the most important characteristic shared by the person-centered theories' (Sheldon and Kasser, 2001, p. 34, original italics; cf Ryan, 1995).

This 'growth-based assumption'—what Will Schutz calls 'the assumption of human limitlessness' (Schutz, 1979, p. 26)—means that the central job of the humanistic therapist is to offer the necessary environment for the inherent tendency to growth to express itself; this is understood to encompass whatever self-healing may be necessary to correct earlier styles of growth which may have become counter-productive. We all do the best we possibly can in the circumstances in which we find ourselves; and this can mean that we 'learn' false lessons about the world, ('scripts', in TA terms) based on the small sample provided by our family.

Humanistic therapy's identification of growth as its goal puts it in sharp conflict with the medical model which currently dominates therapeutic provision, and which requires practice to be 'evidence-based' in the sense that its procedures can be shown to alleviate specific symptoms. This is not the place to argue at length the rights and wrongs of the medical approach (for more on this see e.g., Read, Mosher and Bentall, 1994; Totton, 1997; Wampold, 2001; Sanders, 2005); but clearly a growth-focused approach is very different from a symptom-focused one. For example, the first looks to abundance, while the second identifies deficit; the first is open-ended, while the second is narrowly focused. Many humanistic practitioners would agree that, while symptoms do often lessen or disappear during therapy, this is a by-product of the work rather than its primary goal, which is to increase overall well-being and quality of life by reconnecting the client to the sources of their own growth.

Such an approach is also very different from that of psychoanalysis, in practice if not in theory. Analytically influenced work tends to stress compromise, realism, tolerating anxiety, accepting difficulty and ambiguity. While it does not lack openness to joy and creativity, it rarely embraces the full-on, high octane optimism which is a keynote of humanistic work.

How one feels about this difference is a matter, perhaps, of temperament as much as argument.

3 Empowers clients

This position follows on from and is implied by the previous ones: humanistic therapy locates the capacity for healing and growth primarily *within the client herself* (Sanders, 2006), and secondarily within the relationship of client and therapist. Although the therapist may at times know what to suggest, she is not the *source* of healing; not being a medical practitioner or an analogue of one, it is not her job to diagnose and treat, and in fact this sort of activity is antithetical—in the classic humanistic view—to effective therapy.

The emphasis drawn from this tends to be on conscious choice, the ability to control and direct one's own life. For John Rowan, 'the object of therapy is that the client should have more self-control (autonomy, self-determination, spontaneity, access to personal power, etc)' (Rowan, 1998, p. 49). He goes on to stress that 'The one thing I am never—and can never be—responsible for is the client getting better. As soon as I start thinking thoughts like "I am going to cure this client" or "I really want this person to get better", I am getting tangled up in a different role altogether, the role of rescuer' (Rowan, ibid). We shall look in the next chapter at some of the difficulties with this attitude.

The client is encouraged to identify the sorts of decisions they have made about how to live, the beliefs which they have adopted about how the universe works, and to reconsider whether these are really the most useful options available to them. It is commonly though not universally assumed that once someone becomes fully aware (including on an emotional and embodied level) of their core beliefs and decides to change them, it will not be too difficult to do so: 'we have the power to choose' (Whitton, 2003, p. 41).

This sort of approach has obvious implications for the way in which the therapist relates to the client. Richard Mowbray sums up the central humanistic stance:

> The relationship between practitioner and client is a non-hierarchical partnership between adults with different roles rather than the practitioner having the status of a 'healer' and the client regarded as in need of the practitioner's healing actions. Clients are not regarded as sick or unwell, rather they are 'average maturing adults' concerned to 'know themselves', capable of taking responsibility for themselves and of being self-directing. They have sufficient adult functioning—a *'good enough adult'* as Winnicott might have said.
>
> (Mowbray, 1995, p. 184)

Hence, as I mentioned in Chapter One, the professional relationship between therapist and client is seen as essentially a contract between equals, one of whom has a specific need and the other a specific skill, but neither of whom is superior or inferior to the other in terms of power or worth.

4 *Closer to ordinary communicating*

The perception of the client as a responsible adult, and of therapy as a contractual relationship, both tend to move the relational style of humanistic work in a more ordinary and everyday direction. In the psychodynamic world, for example, rigorous attention to transference and counter-transference, and hence to therapeutic boundaries, can produce a careful, hushed and stylised form of communication. I once saw a video of an initial interview between an analytic therapist and a prospective 'patient' which commenced with the therapist's total silence. After a while the uninitiated and uncomfortable client asked 'Should I start talking, then?' 'Is there something else that you feel should happen?' the therapist responded, with an ineffable air of superiority that one could not help but feel would start the relationship off on an irreparably bad footing.

This sort of interaction of course makes sense within the framework of analytic therapy—though even so one might ask for more deftness and sensitivity. To the inexperienced client, however, it makes no sense whatsoever; and goes a long way to justifying Anna Sands' rhetorical question 'Isn't it possible that, particularly in a psychoanalytic therapy, the relationship—the way each person behaves—is, in itself, dysfunctional?' (Sands, 2000, p. 77). *Bad* psychodynamic psychotherapy (or more commonly, psychodynamic counselling) is possibly the worst form of therapeutic practice in existence, because it has at its disposal so many ways of bamboozling and controlling the client.

In cognitive behavioural styles of therapy, the conventions of medical behaviour are equally alien to the ordinary communication of equals, functioning as if calculated to disempower the 'patient'. Humanistic work, in contrast to both psychodynamic and behavioural work, can very often offer something like what Sands describes as a positive contrast to her initial experience of analytic therapy:

> In my second experience of therapy, the relationship was intrinsically pleasant ... It was an adult relationship with a real, receptive person. When I consciously experienced 'inappropriate' transference feelings about my therapist ... I did not become immersed in them and there was enough emotional distance for me to be able to tell her about them. When difficulties arose, it was often because there were problems on both sides. Every effort was made to address them openly and frankly.
> (Sands, 2000, p. 76)

Sands goes on to argue that

> What needs to happen is the easy expression—from a real human being—of an acceptance of the messy, ugly side

of ourselves, an acknowledgement that our grubbiness is
a normal part of human nature. There is then a sense of
acquaintanceship rather than distance.

(Sands, 2000, p. 90)

This view would be shared by many, though not all, humanistic practitioners. There are clear difficulties here with words like 'real' and 'normal': different people have very different ideas about what corresponds to each of these terms.

In humanistic therapy, while transference and countertransference experiences are widely recognised and acknowledged, they are very often seen more as *obstacles* to useful work than as—the usual contemporary analytic view—*the means by which* the work takes place. Hence they are usually far less rigorously treated than in psychodynamic work. I will look at some of the implications of this in Chapter Three.

5 Contactful

While humanistic therapy may be in many ways more like ordinary relating, there are of course crucial differences. It differs from a chat with a friend not—as psychoanalytic work may be perceived—in the direction of *greater distance*, but in the direction of *closer contact*.

'Contact' is a technical term in both Gestalt and Reichian therapy. In both, it refers not only to interpersonal relating, but to our ways of relating with our environment and with our internal world. In all of these contexts, as a metaphor drawn from physical touch, 'contact' emphasises both *connection* and *boundary*: as Fritz Perls nicely puts it, 'contact is the appreciation of differences' (Fritz Perls, quoted in Heckler, 1984, p. 119), and in the same way that in many physical contexts difference (of temperature, of electrical charge, and so on) creates energy, so in relational contexts contact is the energy of that appreciated difference. Contact is thus a quality independent of physical touch; it is what makes the difference, in fact, between touching one's lover or child, and bumping against the person next to one on a commuter train.

As a therapeutic style, then, contact means offering warm, lively closeness—without imposing it: contact is not invasion or merging (Totton, 2005, pp. 173–4). Humanistic therapists almost invariably work face to face, offering frequent eye contact and emotional connectedness. The experience for the client may well be of greater openness, involvement and challenge than they are used to in the rest of their lives; an experience which humanistic therapy sees as likely to stimulate their inherent desire for this sort of experience, which has been repressed through experiences of invasion and/or abandonment.

Armouring and contraction create a state of contactlessness (Reich, 1972): the individual may wear a mask of vitality and sociality, but is fundamentally out of touch with their own somatic and emotional experience, and similarly out of touch with the world around them and with other people. By uninvasively offering the client embodied contact—which may or may not include physical contact, as discussed in section 7 below—the humanistic therapist seeks to reawaken their ability to feel both self and other.

6 Spontaneous and improvising

Although humanistic therapy clearly has a firm theoretical base, the clinical implications of that base strongly support the use of spontaneity and improvisation to further here-and-now relating. Contact, after all, is only sustainable through a spontaneous style of relating; it is killed by a more programmatic approach. Hence humanistic practitioners will tend to pare their theoretical model down to a few core principles when entering the therapy room. Rogerian work, with its three 'core conditions' is the exemplar of this. 'The essence of person-centered therapy is the therapist's dedication to going with the client's direction, at the client's pace and in the client's unique way of being' (Bower and Bozarth, 1988, p. 59).

This commitment implies a focus on *process* rather than on preconceived categories. Arnold Mindell points out that many forms and techniques of therapy will be spontaneously reinvented by therapists and clients who follow the precise detail of what is going on in the room: 'they are spontaneous creations which arise by amplifying events in given channels of the "therapist-client" interaction even when the two are unfamiliar with these therapies' (Mindell, 1989, p. 8).

Humanistic therapists tend to rely a good deal on their own spontaneous responses, which is clearly one way to guarantee authenticity. Trusting spontaneity is not the same thing as relying on impulse, however. For example, Rowan suggests that if a client asks a question like 'What are you feeling about me now?', the best option is:

> Rather than giving an impulsive answer to this—the first thing that pops in your head—or giving a highly controlled answer—a diplomatic reply ... to give a spontaneous answer, reach into your consciousness for all that is going on in you, at every level, and integrate all those feelings, all those considerations, all those values, into your answer.
> (Rowan, 1998, p. 60).

Though expressed in different terms, this is not really very different from the way a contemporary psychoanalyst might respond.

7 Positive attitude to embodiment and emotion

Humanistic therapy as a whole takes a strongly positive attitude towards bodily experience, and the associated area of emotions: as John Rowan says, 'Many of the humanistic techniques start from the body ... the integration of body and mind is crucial to the humanistic practitioner' (Rowan 1998, p. 86). Hence many humanistic practitioners who do not think of themselves as 'body psychotherapists' will nonetheless be very much at ease bringing into awareness and working therapeutically with their clients' embodied experience, feelings, impulses, symptoms, postures and so on.

This attitude derives especially from, and is especially apparent within, Gestalt therapy. 'For Perls, as well as for many modern Gestaltists, body and psyche are identical, denoting two aspects of the same phenomenon … . Illness is seen as a disturbance in the organism's natural tendency to regulate the self' (Clarkson, 1989, p. 18; cf Heron, 1992, pp. 131ff; Schutz, 1979, pp. 17–18). One might point out that 'identical' is importantly different from 'two aspects'; and certainly there is a lack of conceptual rigour in many humanistic formulations of the bodymind concept. But the basic rejection of mind-body dualism, and the inclusion of embodiment in the therapeutic landscape, are clear.

Embodiment can, but does not necessarily, include physical touch between therapist and client. An essentially comfortable and normalizing attitude towards bodies will tend to spill over into touch in social situations; hence humanistic practitioners may need to consciously refrain from touch for it not to occur spontaneously. And many practitioners do indeed regularly hug their clients when they are in distress or in delight, hold their hands, and otherwise interact physically. All but the most incompetent recognise that there is a boundary issue here, and that relaxation around touch needs to exist on *both* sides, not just for the therapist. However in our contemporary culture many people, especially younger ones, are indeed relaxed about touch, and might well find it odder to encounter traditional therapeutic boundaries than not. And beyond this, many humanistic therapists would see it as part of their job description to implicitly encourage and support a greater openness to touch in their clients.

Similarly, humanistic therapy is welcoming and supportive of emotional expression, which is so closely related to embodiment that the same word, 'feeling', can be used for bodily sensation and for emotion. Most humanistic therapists would agree that 'emotional competence is one of the hallmarks of the self-creating person' (Heron, 1992, p. 131); and while in fact probably the great majority of therapists of all persuasions would sign up to this, unlike some other approaches humanistic therapy sees the free *expression* of feelings—what is often known as 'emotional discharge'—as a key route to emotional competence, arguing that if we are sitting on a backlog of emotional charge, we can hardly take an intelligent attitude towards our lives (Totton and Edmondson, 2009, pp. 21ff).

As Claude Steiner says:

> The realm of our feelings is a vast unexplored area for many of us. This world, which many of us avoid, is like a jungle inhabited by dangerous wild animals, which we would rather pretend is not within us or others.
> (Steiner, 1981, p. 221)

As Steiner recognises, this 'dangerous' aspect is not inherent to emotion, but a side effect of its repression.

> Repressed and denied distress distorts behaviour. Once pushed out of consciousness, or more to the point, prevented from crossing its threshold, what were the perfectly valid distress emotions of grief, boredom, fear and anger go sour. They become rank. They coil into twisted forms, which press against the barrier of repression and warp the behaviour of the false self, who thus becomes an unwitting hostage to its own act of repression.
> (Heron, 1992, p. 129)

This picture is similar to Wilhelm Reich's division of human psychophysical structure into three layers: the living core, the false surface layer, and between the two the middle layer of distorted emotion created by repression from the surface layer, and fear of which keeps the surface layer firmly in place (Reich, 1983 [1942], p. 275). Humanistic therapy holds the firm belief that feelings are 'better out than in', and that a free flow of bodily and emotional energies will tend to maximise our well-being.

8 Positive attitude to spirituality

Humanistic therapy has always had an important place for spiritual experience (Rowan, 1993). Rowan, following the ideas of Ken Wilber (e.g., 1996a, 1996b), sees transpersonal therapy as the 'successor' to humanistic therapy (Rowan 1998, p. 14), in the sense that spiritual growth follows on from and depends on the sorts of personal growth that humanistic therapy offers, and which Wilber refers to as the 'centaur' phase of development. Most humanistic therapists take a less programmatic attitude, and speak of human beings as united body, mind and spirit, who can be and need to be approached through each of these channels at particular moments. Grof's influential work on 'spiritual emergency' (1995) suggests that many psychological crises and breakdowns are best understood and supported as potential spiritual breakthroughs.

Unlike most traditional approaches, humanistic psychotherapy generally rejects the opposition between embodiment and spirituality and takes a welcoming view of both. Will Schutz puts it like this:

> [In Eastern approaches] lower center activities, such as sexuality and competition, are foregone so that energy may be channeled into the higher, spiritual centers. I want all centers flowing fully so that sexuality and spirituality, competition and affection, intellect and feeling, all

> function optimally. I see no need and have no wish for the
> suppression of any capacity for the sake of another.
>
> (Schutz 1979, p. 9)

Brian Thorne, a leading figure in Rogerian circles, has written extensively about the relationship between therapy and spirituality (Thorne, 1991, 1998) from a Christian perspective, somewhat unusually for the field. Thorne integrates a deep involvement in conventional religious institutions with a belief in 'the profound interconnectedness of spirituality and sexuality'.

9 Social critique

As I mentioned in the previous chapter, in the 1960s and 1970s humanistic therapy was in many ways in the vanguard of countercultural politics in the USA and the UK. Although this is no longer the case, some of the core values of humanistic work are still inherently critical of the ways in which our society is organised and the values on which it is based.

One simple example is the emphasis on emotional expression and emotional competence which I have discussed above. Humanistic writers frequently emphasise how different this is, even today, from conventional social values:

> People who see the dentist regularly are held up as examples. People who 'break down and cry' are looked on as 'sissies' and weaklings. There is still a social stigma attached to taking emotional care of oneself or to seeking information about how people function as emotional beings.
>
> (Clarkson, 1989, p. 72)

Heckler makes a similar point about contact, which I discussed earlier: 'How strange it seems that, despite its power to heal and inspire, contact plays such a small part in our education and healing professions, to say nothing of our everyday life'

(Heckler 1984, p. 118); and John Heron discusses at length the 'vast social pathology' which he perceives around the ignoring of emotional competence and the suppression of emotional pain (Heron, 1992, pp. 131f).

These examples could be multiplied many times over. More generally, Mearns and Thorne state that 'there can be little doubt that in many ways the person-centred approach is strikingly out of alignment with much that characterises the current culture of the western world' (Mearns and Thorne, 1999, p. 5); and a number of other humanistic therapists would say the same of their own approach. Humanistic therapy and humanistic psychology see themselves as putting forward viewpoints which are very different from those of mainstream society—and, of course, in their view, very much preferable. What has lessened for many people is the degree of optimism about the possibility of introducing these views into the mainstream, and the attraction to social activism as a way of doing so; and this of course reflects an overall shift in society between the 1970s and the present.

However, there is still a minority of humanistic therapists and psychologists who see social activism as a necessary expression of their world-view (Mindell, 1995; Procter, Cooper and Sanders, 2006; Diaz-Laplante, 2007). The Vasconcellos Project, named after and inspired by a veteran California State Senator who is also a veteran of humanistic therapies, has coined the slogan 'the Politics of Trust', arguing that

> Conditioned by the belief that humanity is by nature flawed and inclined toward wrongdoing, most public policy today emphasizes restricting, controlling, and punishing. Instead, society should focus upon liberating and empowering each person to achieve her or his potential. This is a vision of politics and governance that truly serves the human interest … . Politics is about power. Power is not just about controlling others. Humanistic power is

about recognizing the life force within us and trusting the human heart to hear the direction it would lead. How we do power changes lives, and the politics we practice is based on who we are.

(Vasconcellos Project, n.d.)

10 Experiential paradigm of practice and research

As I have mentioned several times, humanistic *therapy* is twinned with the academic discipline of humanistic *psychology*. But the principles of humanistic therapy necessarily affect the ways in which the discipline is conducted: there are aspects of traditional academic psychology which conflict directly with humanistic ideas. The primary issue here is around 'qualitative' as opposed to 'quantitative' research method: that is, research that focuses on the complexity of human experience rather than, in the classic hard science approach, seeking a way to turn that experience into numbers.

The first humanistic psychologists, including both Rogers and Maslow, tended to accept quantitative methods uncritically (Aanstoos, 2003, p. 124). It was only later that the phenomenological basis of humanistic work began to inform a more radical approach (Giorgi, 1970; Giorgi, Ashworth and de Koning, 1986); this was eventually taken up by Rogers (1985), who became an advocate for qualitative research. According to Aanstoos (2003, p. 124), this research approach is now achieving 'rigor and depth ... capable of meeting the daunting challenge of explicating human experience'.

There are however other humanistic researchers who believe that it is both possible and important to apply quantitative methods to their work. Sheldon and Kasser argue that '"quantitative methodology" and "sensitive humanism" can be in harmony rather than in opposition to one another and ... bringing them together can yield substantial new understanding and explanatory power for all of psychology' (Sheldon and Kasser, 2001, p. 33). So, for example, they focus on the concept of 'intrinsic motivation'—otherwise known as self-directedness—and explore how an emphasis on intrinsic rather than extrinsic goals is reflected in quantitative measures of wellbeing, finding a significant positive relationship between the two (ibid, pp. 44–5).

This and other work supports the view that humanistic ideas *can* be tested and supported by traditional quantitative methods. However there is still a strong argument for developing methodologies which more closely reflect humanistic beliefs, rather than struggling to fit the Procrustean bed of conventional science. A leading figure here has been John Heron, whose model of 'cooperative inquiry' (Heron, 1981, 1996)—which re-identifies the 'experimental subject' as a peer participant in the research, an approach which is also called 'human inquiry' or 'participatory' or 'new paradigm' research—has been taken up by a number of other figures particularly in the UK (Reason and Rowan, 1981; Reason, 1988).

The experiential approach to humanistic research is closely paralleled in clinical work, where there is a strong emphasis on what works rather than on what makes the best theoretical patterns. However, 'what works' in this context is very different from 'evidence-based practice': while the latter restricts its concept of 'evidence' to double blind quantitative trials, humanistic therapy has generally found its evidence of effectiveness in concrete clinical encounters. Each practitioner, whether or not they teach or publish, is supported in following their own experience of what works or doesn't work in their own consulting room. Notions like congruence and authenticity of course demand that the therapist be able to improvise outside the box of standard therapeutic techniques.

Conclusion

In my view these ten points—which could be extended and varied in many ways—clearly establish the value and significance of humanistic psychotherapy and counselling.

In the 1950s and 1960s when the various approaches were becoming widely known in the United States, they faced a largely moribund and reactionary psychoanalytic establishment and an equally lethargic academic psychology; their contrasting energy and vitality was swiftly apparent to many people, and coincided with a general societal swing towards innovation and personal freedom.

The current situation is very different, both within the field of psychological practice and in society as a whole. Partly in reaction to the tremendous threats which it faces (and I am thinking more of future shock, climate change and environmental degradation than of 'terror'), society in the west is more conservative, more timid, more oriented towards safety and conformity. At the same time, the peers/rivals of humanistic therapy are in a far healthier state now then they were then: psychoanalysis, despite or because of its lowered cultural status, has been revitalised, particularly by the relational trend in analytic work (Mitchell and Aron, 1999), while cognitive behavioural therapy, rightly or wrongly seen as the most effective approach to the psychological symptoms which plague our society, is also in a ferment of internal creativity, largely around its relationship to mindfulness practices (Brantley, 2007; Hayes, 2007; Segal, Williams and Teasdale, 2002). However, humanistic therapy still has unique and precious qualities to offer; and at their heart is its straightforward emphasis on simple human relationship as the primary source of healing and empowerment.

CHAPTER THREE

Weaknesses of humanistic therapies

This chapter is the difficult twin of the previous one, casting a sceptical light on the features which were more positively spun in Chapter Two. Again, in some cases I myself may be less critical than the arguments which I present; in general, the most accurate picture will, I feel, fall somewhere between the two chapters. Criticisms are sometimes accompanied by extenuating arguments. The ten weaknesses I will explore—which, again, correspond to the ten strengths of the previous chapter—are as follows:

- A Pollyanna complex
- A denial of pathology
- Giving undue responsibility to clients
- Missing transferential issues
- Boundary problems
- Glorifying impulsiveness
- Taking a negative attitude towards rationality and theory
- Prone to mysticism and 'uplift'
- Out of the mainstream
- Weak on research

Pollyanna complex

Humanistic therapy is vulnerable to accusations of being over-positive and over-optimistic about people's potential for happiness and successful living. After all, the evidence is all around us that people live unhappy and unproductive lives. If it is true that 'the person moves inherently towards self-regulation and away from being controlled' (Bozarth, 1998, p. 30) then why are so many people in this world so tightly controlled by so few?

Writing from a sympathetic perspective, Linda Riebel says:

> Superficial acquaintance with humanistic psychology can lead to the impression that it is unrealistic on two counts: The pursuit of the healthy and the extraordinary is taken to imply a neglect of the maladjusted and neurotic, and the pursuit of the individual's growth is taken to imply a neglect of social responsibility. More precisely, emphasis on the positive potential aspects of human nature (humanistic theory) and the release of these aspects into actuality (humanistic practice) are questioned by people who are concerned about the unproductive or abnormal aspects of the individual and the destructive capacities of society.
>
> (Riebel, 1982, pp. 349–50)

It may not only be a 'superficial' acquaintance that gives this impression, though the first point seems to me stronger than the second: relative to other therapies, humanistic therapy if anything shows a greater concern with 'social responsibility', as we saw in the previous chapter. But just as its perspective on the individual is optimistic, so its social perspective tends to be utopian; in neither arena does it meet the questions raised by those who are less warm and fuzzy about the human capacity for evil, injustice and misery (Geller, 1982).

Denies pathology

As well as believing that people have an unlimited potential for growth, humanistic therapy also believes that, just as we are now, we are basically and fundamentally OK (Harris, 1967). This clearly distinguishes it from models which focus on 'mental illness', currently supposed to be reaching 'epidemic' proportions in the Western world. But even much less medically-oriented approaches will often acknowledge that people can be in a bad state which to all intents and purposes is structural in nature, and which has—even if the terms are, rightly, avoided—what amounts to a recognisable and consistent etiology, prognosis and treatment.

Humanistic therapy has a fraught relationship with such ideas as these. Speaking of Gestalt, Clarkson points out that it has 'traditionally rejected such a dehumanisation of patients. To label people "anal-retentive" or "manic-depressive" can be to strip them of the unique ways in which they have chosen to give meaning to their existence' (Clarkson, 1989, p. 23). However, she also acknowledges that 'recognition of repeated patterns in human behaviour (whether momentary or long-term) is ... intrinsic to a holistic approach' (Clarkson, ibid).

The difficulty for humanistic therapists is to find a comfortable balance between on the one hand acknowledging that all experienced practitioners of course recognise patterns to the problems which people bring, and on the other hand maintaining as a core position that 'each person is unique' (Clarkson, 1989, p. 62), that 'the authority about a person rests in the person rather than in an outside expert' (Bozarth, 1998, p. 127), and that 'to diagnose someone is to label them. And labelling does harm to people' (Rowan, 1998, p. 23). The next phrase of Rowan's statement makes a very helpful point: he argues that 'labelling does harm to people, *even when the labels are correct*' (Rowan, ibid, my italics). In other words, one does not even have to invalidate the diagnostic categories in order to argue that they are unhelpful, simply because they block the therapeutic relationship by suggesting that the therapist, rather than the client, is the expert on the client's problems.

Despite all this, however, and despite very little shift in humanistic therapy's viewpoint, a lot more assessment and diagnosis is going on now in humanistic circles than was formerly the case. This seems to be primarily because of external pressure, ultimately financial: both the NHS and insurance companies demand a diagnosis of pathology in order to approve (pay for) therapeutic work, and this is also becoming the norm in voluntary agencies (Sanders, 2005).

As a result, many humanistic theoreticians are developing their own versions of conventional diagnostic categories—primarily those used in DSM IV (American Psychiatric Association, 1994). For example, there is a paper on 'A System of Gestalt Diagnosis of Borderline, Narcissistic, and Schizoid Adaptations' (Greenberg, 2003); and another very influential one on how the traditional pathologies—schizoid, hysteric, and so on—can be understood in TA terms (Ware, 1983). Joines (1986) takes up Ware's system into his own TA approach, Redecision Therapy, but tries to treat the six types as just varieties of people, neutral with respect to health or pathology (Joines, 1986, p. 153), and hence renames them—schizoids become 'Creative Daydreamers', hysterics 'Enthusiastic Overreactors', and so on; terms like 'overreactor' demonstrate how hard it actually is to avoid pathologization.

Rogerians have held out most strongly against pathology and diagnosis, since such concepts are directly inimical to their whole approach (Sanders, 2006, pp. 46ff); however, in another paper Sanders questions why 'counsellors have abdicated the radical position' of Rogerian work in the 1950s and 'become tacit supporters of the medical psychiatric position' (Sanders, 2005, p. 21). Ironically, the editors' introduction to the volume in which this paper appears argues for the need to 'build bridges' and 'speak the language of psychiatry and psychology' (Joseph and Worsley, 2005, pp. 1, 7).

Misses transferential issues

Measured in relation to psychodynamic work, humanistic therapists tend to handle transferential issues in a relaxed, offhand, or even slapdash way. Rowan rightly suggests that this stems not from incompetence but from unwillingness:

> I do get the feeling that most humanistic people don't like the idea of transference and countertransference going on in the relationship between therapist and client. Why should this be?
> I think the main reason is that we believe that the exclusive reliance on transference by a therapist means a very narrow and one-sided imbalance in the relationship.
> (Rowan, 1998, p. 120)

The complex relationship between the first and second paragraphs of this quotation is instructive. 'Most humanistic people' becomes 'we', and 'the idea of transference' becomes 'the exclusive reliance on transference'; it is as though the dispassionate observer in the first paragraph becomes a raging partisan in the second. And this does indeed seem to be a passionate issue for many humanistic therapists: there is almost an allergic reaction to the idea of transference interpretation, primarily because it seems to place too much power in the therapist's hands, since they have the power to interpret any criticism from the client as 'just transference' (Sands, 2000, pp. 64ff).

While this is perhaps an accurate concern about some forms of psychodynamic practice, it does seem to represent a rather out of date view of what analytic therapists get up to. In particular, it emphasises transference much more than countertransference, negating the contemporary realisation (Mitchell and Aron, 1999) that the unconscious of the therapist is as much involved in the relationship as that of the client, and that client and therapist are in many ways equal partners in finding their way through the multiple entanglements and enmeshments of their encounter. It further ignores the idea (e.g., Jacobs, 2005) of *enactment*: that a very powerful way—perhaps sometimes the only way—of accessing traumatic experience is for it to be played out symbolically between client and therapist. (For a body-centred account of enactment, see Soth, 2005.)

In contrast to all this, Rowan's summing up of transference harks back to the simple picture, which Freud presented in his early analytic writings a century ago, of transference as a *mistake* on the part of the client:

> The perception of the therapist's behaviour, both verbal and nonverbal, may very easily be diverted ... into a sexual pattern, into an affiliative pattern, into a dependency pattern. ... there is really no way of totally preventing such misconceptions and such misperceptions.
> (Rowan, 1998, p. 68)

Later in the book, Rowan seems to think again, and presents something much closer to a psychoanalytic critique of humanistic attitudes: '*The therapist holds all the aces, whether s/he wants them or not*. This is the crucial truth about transference, which the Freudians are aware of and the humanistic therapists run away from' (Rowan, 1998, p. 121; original italics).

This realisation that the therapist *cannot help* being the object of the client's feelings about power and powerlessness, acceptance and non-acceptance, is one which humanistic practitioners tend to resist. It runs counter to their optimistic and voluntaristic view of the world, which says—in caricature—that if we all just *want* the right thing and *try hard* to achieve it, then everything will turn out well. As I argue later on in this chapter, the concept of the unconscious is antithetical to this viewpoint.

Gives undue responsibility to clients

The allergic reaction which I have described to transference interpretations—or indeed, in some forms of humanistic work, to any response which suggests that the therapist understands something about the client which the client does not—inevitably leaves a great deal of responsibility with the client. This can be seen as an abdication of power to help, rather than as an empowerment of the client: after all, even if they are the best authority on their own issues, they may well need a good deal of support in *recognising* their own authority, and this support may include challenging their resistance and avoidance of self-knowledge.

This is putting the case in the most humanistic way possible; for many therapists who are either medically or analytically orientated, it will seem obvious that the practitioner brings expert knowledge to the situation, and that to withhold that expertise would be irresponsible. And in fact it is not unknown for the client of a humanistic practitioner, as much as the client of a psychodynamic practitioner, to feel that they are being left high and dry by their therapist's non-intervention. (There may well be a transference component to this feeling in either client—but will the humanistic practitioner be willing to identify it?)

There is a deeper issue here, around the philosophy of autonomy which grounds humanistic therapy. The prominent humanistic therapist Maureen O' Hara in fact developed a critique of the assumption that autonomy is *the* desirable state of being, suggesting that it is culturally conditioned and in some ways illusory and damaging, since human beings necessarily depend upon each other (O'Hara, 1989). Similarly, Leonard Geller (1982) argues that the ideas of Maslow and Rogers are based on the atomized, dehumanised individual produced by modern Western culture, and hence give ideological support to that experience of self.

In a clinical context, this can mean that people's problems are understood in terms of their personal psychology, rather than in the context of the social and economic institutions which affect them. In similar vein, Howard Clinebell (1981, p. 180) writes about Gestalt therapy's tendency toward 'hyperindividualism', quoting Fritz Perls' well-known 'Gestalt Prayer':

> I do my thing and you do your thing. I am not in this world to live up to your expectations and you are not in this world to live up to mine. You are you and I am I, and if, by chance, we find each other, it's beautiful. If not, it can't be helped.
>
> (Perls, 1969b, p. 4)

Despite the attractiveness of this, as Clinebell says:

> A weakness in gestalt is an underemphasis on the responsibility of truly liberated persons to strive to change the oppressive structures of society. Peris was keenly aware of the social sources of diminished growth. It is from the collective psychosis of our culture that we learn our phoney, deadening games. But in response to this awareness he offered only the image of the autonomous, self-directed individual standing against the insanities of society.
>
> (Clinebell, 1981, p. 180)

Obsession with the individual is a danger for all forms of psychotherapy, of course, not only humanistic work; but in the case of humanists, there is a link to New Age ways of thinking about responsibility which, by taking notions of autonomy to an absurd extreme, can end up blaming the individual for their own oppression. Will Schutz expresses this position very bluntly:

> I choose my whole life and I always have. I choose my behavior, my feelings, my thoughts, my illnesses, my body, my reactions, my spontaneity, my death.

Some of these choices I choose to be aware of and some
I choose not to be aware of.
(Schutz, 1979, p. 31)

Unlike some others, Schutz is not afraid to follow through the full logical implications of this stance and say that 'social minorities are oppressed only if they allow themselves to be put in a position they call oppression' (ibid, p. 40),and that 'a rape "victim" is choosing to be raped and a rapist is choosing to rape. They collude to bring about the outcome' (ibid, p. 49). In fact he goes on to quote a disturbing piece of writing by a woman 'taking responsibility' for being raped as a five year old child (ibid, pp. 50–3).

This sort of thinking was barely acceptable in the 1970s, and in fact came under strong attack from other humanistic therapists: for example, Claude Steiner argues that although 'the pursuit of happiness is a rational endeavour and a great deal depends on our attitudes and actions', when this is developed into 'a mindless belief in our absolute power to control our own destiny, it can justifiably be thought of as having become an idiotic notion' (Steiner, 1981, p. 79). Nowadays, few people would explicitly argue for the responsibility of the victim. However, the theoretical position that 'I create my reality' is still commonly asserted in humanistic circles, and having granted that premise there is no clear way to escape Schutz's conclusion. The belief that we individually and solipsistically create our own worlds, if naively applied, can have a damaging effect on clients, actually *dis*empowering them rather than the opposite; and, of course, it undermines any sort of social activism.

John Rowan has an intelligent commentary on these ideas (Rowan, 1998, pp. 110–112), where he rightly points out the significant difference between saying '*I* create my world' and '*you* create your own world' or '*he/she* creates their own world'. Although, for unspecified reasons, he views 'I create my world' as 'the most productive stance in therapy' (ibid, p. 110), he argues that the third-person statement is 'a denial of solidarity, a negation of community ... not conducive to growth at all' (ibid, p. 111), and that the second-person statement can tend towards either the first or third person connotations depending on its empathic context. Another way of saying this is that I only have the right to make this statement about myself, not to impose it on others.

The general emphasis in humanistic work on individual choice and responsibility may be unhelpful for those numerous clients for whom such ideas are actually part of their problem—people who present themselves as rational and responsible adults, but perhaps badly need to admit their helplessness and anxiety. And many humanistic practitioners are of course well aware of this. However TA, for example, still places at the centre of its system the concept of the Adult ego-state, described as 'behaviours, thoughts and feelings which are a direct response to the here-and-now' (Stewart and Joines, 1987, p. 12); which implicitly states that to be anxious and emotional for historical reasons is less than adult.

Boundary problems

The same emphasis on individual choice and responsibility, on 'Sufficient Available Functioning Adult Autonomy' (Mowbray, 1995, p. 183) as the default assumption, can also problematise the question of appropriate therapeutic boundaries. Given that humanistic therapy, as we saw in Chapter Two, tends to offer warm and close contact, it is crucial that the therapist is able to recognise and respond to any reluctance in the client and back off sufficiently to establish a safe space to work in.

Many clients, however, do not give clear signals about the boundaries they need—because they feel ashamed, think the therapist must know best, are paralysed with anxiety, or are unconscious of their own feelings. A therapist who trusts their clients to know and express what they want, and who also habitually offers intimacy and closeness, is treading on dangerous ground. Humanistic practitioners are perhaps especially vulnerable to charismatic over-generosity, shifting boundaries to 'meet the client's needs' (for example around session times, phonecalls and texts, or fees) in ways that may actually be destabilising for them. (For a psychoanalytic critique of such flexibility, see Smith, 1991, or the more moderate arguments of Casement, 1985.)

Most experienced practitioners, of course, are well aware of these pitfalls (see e.g., Rowan, 1998, pp. 55–6). But there are undeniably a certain number of rogue elephants in the humanistic world, long-established, charismatic therapists who do not believe that the normal rules apply to them, and who trust in their own boundless self-belief to see them through any difficulty. Often they get away with stretching the boundaries, because they are gifted therapists of great personal genuineness—though even so their clients may end up in a state of unhelpful confluence and dependence. But once in a while something really bad happens which could have been avoided by simple common sense and self-discipline.

Glorifies impulsiveness

The 'rogue elephants' I have just described believe profoundly that following their impulses (which they tend to call 'therapeutic intuition', 'heart wisdom', etc.) will be therapeutically productive, and this attitude, tempered to a greater or lesser extent by humility and self-examination, permeates humanistic therapy. We can even see some traces of it in Rowan's very measured account quoted in the previous chapter, specifically cast as an alternative to impulsiveness, of how to respond to a difficult direct question from a client:

> Rather than giving an impulsive answer to this—the first thing that pops in your head—or giving a highly

> controlled answer—a diplomatic reply ... to give a spontaneous answer, reach into your consciousness for all that is going on in you, at every level, and integrate all those feelings, all those considerations, all those values, into your answer.
>
> (Rowan, 1998, p. 60)

Notice that the injunction is to 'reach into your *consciousness*', as if what we are aware of in ourselves, even through the most exhaustive cataloguing, is equivalent to the whole picture. As we see over and over again humanistic psychotherapy is deeply prone to trust conscious intention, whether in the client or in the practitioner. And the combination of trusting consciousness and privileging authenticity can at worst—despite Rowan's disavowal—produce a sort of glorification of impulsiveness. Certainly our impulses are important; but generally they are better used as a source of information than as guidance for action.

Negative attitude to rationality and theory

Humanistic therapy manages at times to combine a rejection of the unconscious with a rejection as well of rational consciousness. Its rehabilitation of feeling and sensation, undoubtedly a vital rebalancing of Western cultural priorities, can in turn itself become one-sided. Certainly pretty much all those drawn to therapy as a career who are also characterologically most comfortable with emotion and sensation will end up in the humanistic camp.

This tendency is certainly no more extreme than the corresponding privilege given by certain other schools to reason or to intuition. And it is probably healthy for the whole range of human types to be represented in the range of therapy and counselling modalities. However, for this to be maximally useful a degree of self-awareness is required in practitioners, an ability to identify their own preferences as just that, *preferences*—and hence, an ability either to refer on certain clients with very different styles, or, ideally, to widen one's own range to meet them.

This self-awareness is not always found among humanistic practitioners, who may be content simply to privilege the body and the emotions over thinking (other practitioners are of course prone to parallel blind spots). This is a problem identified by some humanistic practitioners themselves (e.g., Rowan, 1998, p. 107), and generates a widespread tendency to intellectual fuzziness within humanistic work. There are humanistic theoreticians, of course; but there is a sharp division between those whose theoretical work is essentially pragmatic and concrete, like Carl Rogers, and those who claim a vast but cloudy lineage for humanistic psychology including figures like Socrates, Ficino, Nietszche, Husserl and Merleau-Ponty (e.g., Moss, 2001). This latter group seems to me unconvincing, and generally lacking intellectual crispness, as if the incantation of famous names can substitute for close reasoning.

Overall, many would say that humanistic psychology is not a coherent intellectual structure. Maureen O'Hara, one of the founding figures of humanistic therapy, asserted in 1989 that:

> Even after 25 years, humanistic psychology is not yet a discipline but is what Kuhn refers to as "preparadigmatic". It is an amorphous field of enquiry in which there are no general axioms, no consensus as to the important questions or standards of evaluation, and wherein quite different forms of utterance are made about the nature of human reality.
>
> (O'Hara, 1989, p. 263)

One striking example of this is that, according to Dave Mearns, there were no books devoted to Rogerian therapy training prior to 1997 (Mearns, 2003, p. 56).

More recently, the prominent humanistic writer David Cain asks his colleagues: *'Do we continue to suffer from an outdated and negative reputation associated with touchy-feely and anti-intellectual attitudes, with encounter groups, fringe therapies and lack of scientific rigor?'* (Cain, 2003, p. 23; original italics). He answers in the affirmative, quoting some humanistic workshop titles—'"Digital Aboriginal," "Cosmos, Dream, Eros and Psyche," "The Pleasure and Price of Remaining Unaware," "An Introduction to Deep Fun," "On Becoming A Practical Mystic," and "Heartmath Solution and Inner Quality Management"'—and suggesting that 'we may continue to be seen as fuzzy, soft-headed thinkers willing to entertain the most outlandish of ideas or practices' (Cain, ibid).

Whatever we may think of this, it is undeniable that intellectual rigour is in short supply in humanistic circles, with many theoretical incoherences and inconsistencies left unaddressed. I will take as an example the concept of the Adult ego-state in TA, which I have already mentioned. On what grounds are 'behaviours, thoughts and feelings which are direct responses to the here-and-now' (Stewart and Joines, 1987, p. 12) identified with 'using all the resources available to me as a grown-up human person' (ibid, p. 4)? Surely there are many other resources, of memory, desire, fantasy, anticipation, theory-forming, even dissociation, available to grown-up people?

There is an odd asymmetry in the way TA defines the three ego-states: the Child is about 'return[ing] to ways of behaving, thinking and feeling which I used when I was a child', and the Parent about 'copy[ing]' the ways of behaving, etc., used by parents and carers. But while these two ego-states are defined by reference to other times and people, the Adult is circularly defined as behaving like 'a grown-up human person'—the Adult behaves like an adult! (All from Stewart and Joines, p. 4).

TA seems to be using an unexamined set of assumptions about what adults *should* be like to define this ego-state; and calling it by the name Adult builds these assumptions into the system. But perhaps adults *should* be more like children, for example? The way TA describes the Adult as existing in the here-and-now could be seen as rather like an animal—which is not meant to be derogatory to animals. Actually TA seems to believe that adult human beings need all three ego-states; in which case it makes even less sense to name one of them Adult. This is only one of many possible examples from across the range of humanistic modalities where greater intellectual rigour and questioning of unexamined assumptions would be desirable.

Prone to mysticism and 'uplift'

If rationality is downplayed and even discouraged, then humanistic therapy's friendliness towards the transpersonal will tend easily to lose its balance. Indeed, there are those who argue that this imbalance is at the root of humanistic work, that, for instance, the actualizing tendency is in effect conceptualised as an 'occult force', and that humanistic psychology can never go beyond a romantic and sentimental account of humanity (McMullen, 1982). McMullen places humanistic psychology in the context of the New Age flight from reason, alongside systems like magic and astrology.

How one feels about this rather depends on how one feels about magic, astrology and so on. It seems clear that many more humanistic practitioners than psychoanalytic or CBT practitioners are also sympathetic to New Age ideas, and vice versa; the same is no doubt true for clients. This in itself is surely not a problem; but problems will arise if the practitioner preaches these or any other ideas to their clients, or insists on interpreting the client's issues within such frameworks.

There is equally a possible problem when it is the client who brings a magical or mystical framework to the therapy. When someone organises their perception of relationships and life issues in terms of, say, past lives or spirit guides, it is certainly not appropriate to contradict them; but nor is it necessarily helpful to agree with them. Whatever the client's ideological framework, probably the most helpful contribution of the therapist is to treat it as a potentially helpful *metaphor*. This is obviously much easier to do if the framework is one with which we can sympathise, but which we do not actually share.

One important example of a New Age framework is the idea, discussed above, that 'I create my own reality'. I have myself had many clients who produce this notion in therapy; occasionally it seems useful, offering (as in the Claude Steiner quotation above) an incentive to positive attitude and effort, but much more often it functions as a justification for self-attack or fatalism. As so often, it is not *the idea itself* which is important so much as what the client—or the therapist—does with it.

Out of the mainstream

I said in Chapter Two that some of humanistic therapy's core values go against the mainstream of our society as currently constituted. Probably the majority of humanistic practitioners are at ease with this; but there are an increasing number of voices arguing that humanistic therapy should row back into the mainstream as rapidly as possible.

The main reason given for this view is that humanistic therapy lacks appropriate influence on the wider world. David Cain puts it like this:

> Many of our founding fathers and mothers were mavericks who advanced bold ideas that ran counter to but transformed mainstream psychology. ... Many of us continue to value our role as firebrands, gadflies, radicals, and mavericks. However, it seems fair to ask how our continuing maverick attitudes serve or impair our development and progress. Many humanistic psychologists

have antipathetic or extremely ambivalent relationships with mainstream psychology ... Our "us-against-them" attitude has resulted in our being on the outside looking in, complaining about our lack of recognition.

(Cain, 2003, p. 19)

The use of the 'maverick' metaphor is revealing: a maverick is a calf unbranded with an owner's mark (the mark of Cain?). Cain suggests that 'our publications remain sparse in mainstream journals, and most of our texts, though of excellent quality, have modest impact and are generally not adopted as graduate texts' (Cain, 2003, p. 17)—something which is clearly galling for him.

From a slightly different point of view, Dave Mearns characterises the countercultural flavour of humanistic therapy—specifically, Rogerian therapy—as 'naive', and argues that it renders practitioners powerless in relation to institutions

It may not be true of other humanistic psychologists, but person-centered specialists tend to show an incredible naiveté in relation to institutions. Indeed, sometimes they even expect the institution to be "person centered." The reality is that institutions, logically, tend to be "institution centered." If we do not accept this fundamental premise, it is extremely difficult to work effectively in relation to an institution.

(Mearns, 2003, p. 57)

This is the same position taken by Joseph and Worsley in relation to the issue of psychopathology, discussed above: that person-centred therapy becomes 'isolated' and 'marginalised' if it disagrees with mainstream stances and refuses to use mainstream language (Joseph and Worsley, 2005, p. 7).

Similar arguments are often made in relation to any nonconformist position—that as an outsider one has no power to change things, and that it is more effective to work for change from within. The counter-argument, of course, is that working from within one tends to get bogged down in detail and imperceptibly to mislay one's original ideals. As I put it some years ago, 'while we are altering the system, it is also altering us: working away subtly at our sense of priorities, our language, our style' (Totton, 1997, p. 115). Holding the 'extreme' position will probably never succeed as such, but it may well shift the centre over in our direction. Which choice one makes is a matter of personal style; certainly, there is room for both working from within and working from without.

Weak on research

Interestingly, Taylor takes the converse viewpoint to the criticisms outlined in the last section, arguing in relation to research that:

> Most humanistic and transpersonal psychologists remain unaware that their ideas have crept into mainstream personality diagnosis. As well, they do not normally engage in this kind of empirical work themselves. Rather, they advocate the centrality of their work for psychology as a whole and tend to peripheralize the importance of what most other psychologists are concerned with. Meanwhile, their own venue has been pre-empted now by these genetic researchers in psychiatry who have put forward a more sophisticated and empirically based picture of the whole personality that includes everything the humanistic and transpersonal psychologists have been advocating plus more.
>
> (Taylor, 1999, p. 14)

On examination, this is not strictly the converse of the 'out of the mainstream' argument: Taylor is saying that humanistic researchers tend solipsistically to place themselves at the centre and (like many nonconformist minorities) ignore what everyone else is actually doing. A similar view can be taken of the dogmatic preference for qualitative rather than quantitative research which is common in humanistic psychology. Sheldon and Kasser argue that

> "quantitative methodology" and "sensitive humanism" can be in harmony rather than in opposition to one another and, further, that bringing them together can yield substantial new understanding and explanatory power for all of psychology.
>
> (Sheldon and Kasser 2001, p. 33)

In the paper quoted, they offer a model example of the application of quantitative methods to humanistic topics, using what they describe (pp. 30–1) as 'state-of-the-art quantitative methodologies, longitudinal designs, and causal modeling techniques' to investigate and support the hypothesis that 'well-being and relationship quality are ... better when people orient toward *intrinsic* values such as intimacy, community, and growth, rather than *extrinsic* values such as status, money, and image' (ibid, p. 31).

Driven largely by the demands of the marketplace and the need to compete effectively with other therapeutic modalities, some humanists have increasingly sought to create research programmes which will offer 'hard' support for the humanistic therapies. However, they are faced with the difficulty that double-bind efficacy studies, currently portrayed as the gold standard of psychotherapy research, 'violates most of the key values and assumptions of humanistic psychotherapy' (Vermeersch and Lambert 2003, p. 108) through their emphasis on manualization and the assumption that clients can be standardized and treated as interchangeable.

Howard, Moras, Brill, Martinovich, and Lutz (1996) introduced the concept and technique of 'client-focused research', a longitudinal study of how particular methodologies affect particular clients, in an attempt to produce a research paradigm which is even handed between the whole range of therapies and does not conflict with the core values of any of them. This attempt has had only very limited results. Friedman and Macdonald (2006) argue that testing and assessment can be consistent with the values of humanistic therapy: 'For those who want to continue practice in a humanistic mode, there will be increasing pressure to provide evidence of the effectiveness and nonharmfulness of these services. Thoroughly articulated assessment formulations that are supported by test results can be extremely useful in such times' (p. 527).

Wertz sums up the negative ways in which humanistic psychology is seen in relation to academic psychology (after an almost equally long list of positives):

> The movement is more a common sense attitude of valuing and respecting people, often amounting to sappy sentimentality, than a scientific discipline. The movement's protests outweigh its positive contributions. The critiques of mainstream psychology are now outdated and no longer apply. The movement has had more impact on psychotherapeutic practice than on the explanation of behavior. The movement is vague in its objectives, fragmented in its achievements, and contains no discernible principles of unity. Rigorous research methods have been lacking. The introduction of new topics, which should be and have been studied in traditional ways, does not revolutionize psychology. The topics of mainstream psychology have not been researched. The theories have not been defined and tested sufficiently according to scientific standards. The promise to interrelate psychology with the humanities has not been full-filled. Many of these problems are attributed to the movement's large proportion of

practitioners, as opposed to researchers, and its failure to establish a place for itself in academic institutions.

(Wertz, 1998, p. 45)

Conclusion: The elephant in the room

There are many areas of overlap between humanistic and psychodynamic work; despite differences of emphasis, they are recognisably engaged in the same task of helping people get to know and accept themselves better, in the expectation that this will improve their lives in many ways. Hence they are much more clearly aligned with each other than either is with CBT, which is closely focused on the alleviation of symptoms rather than on self-knowledge. (This is beginning to change with the development of mindfulness-based approaches to CBT; see e.g., Hayes, 2007.)

However there is one central difference between humanistic and psychodynamic therapies, which some readers may already have been wanting me to focus on. Overall and with exceptions, humanistic therapists are not very interested in the unconscious. They do not necessarily deny its existence (though some do); but by and large they do not really understand the concept, minimise its importance, and are deeply suspicious of therapeutic styles which highlight it.

We have already seen some of this in humanistic therapy's attitude to transference and countertransference: acknowledgement that it exists, but a general unenthusiasm for working with it or taking it too seriously. Transference is widely seen as something to *avoid* if at all possible; Rowan says regretfully that 'there is really no way of totally preventing such misconceptions and such misperceptions' (Rowan, 1998, p. 68). One almost feels that unconscious material is also seen as something to be avoided if possible. And the Freudian understanding of the unconscious as actually *unavailable* to consciousness, rather than just temporarily ignored, is not widely grasped by humanistic therapists. For example, Will Schutz says 'Although these meanings are virtually identical, I prefer to use the terms "aware" and "unaware" instead of "conscious" and "unconscious"' (Schutz, 1979, p. 34). From an analytic point of view, the two sets of terms are in no way interchangeable: I may be *unaware* of the time, but I am certainly not *unconscious* of it, resisting knowledge of it and unable to take in information from clocks.

As I have indicated, this dismissive attitude towards the unconscious is not usually argued out explicitly, but is more of a background atmosphere; however, it does permeate the humanistic field, and I suggest that it is behind several of the problems with humanistic work which I have outlined in this chapter. If one is suspicious of and unenthusiastic about the notion of unconscious feelings, then it is very hard to work well with transference and countertransference; the motivation for keeping firm boundaries is greatly lessened; we will tend to take things more at face value, and hence to believe more in the 'responsible adult' with which many of our clients try to present us.

I suggest that the motives behind humanistic practitioners' aversion to the unconscious are in fact closely bound up with these limitations (as one may see them from a psychodynamic viewpoint). Humanistic therapy is the standard bearer for personal empowerment, personal responsibility. The unconscious, as Freudians have been saying for over a century (beginning with Freud's famous comparison between his own work and that of Copernicus and Darwin—Freud 1917, pp. 139–41), *decentres* personal awareness, identifies it as just one part of or place within the psyche—a much smaller place, in fact, than the aspects of the psyche outside our personal awareness. While it is not impossible to synthesise this with a picture of personal empowerment, doing so is not a simple matter. Hence the deep suspicion with which most humanists view the unconscious;

and hence, perhaps, some of the key limitations of humanistic practice.

And as I have also already hinted, the person whom humanistic therapy wants to empower is not only the client, but also the practitioner. Humanistic therapists often resist swallowing the bitter pill of their own helplessness. As I quoted Eric Berne saying in the first triumphant flush of his new way of working, 'We don't want patients to make progress ... We want them to get well' (Languth, 1966). Fully to recognise the unconscious is to come up against the sheer difficulty of change, and the many pitfalls that get in the way of the humanistic practitioner's fantasy of curing her clients by loving them enough.

CHAPTER FOUR

How to move forward?

Having explored both the strengths and the weaknesses of the humanistic therapies, it is time to offer some tentative suggestions as to how things might move forward. I want again to offer a list of points—only six rather than ten as in the previous two chapters, and this time I will frame them as questions for discussion, rather than as statements.

- Is the autonomous status of humanistic therapy still important?
- What, if any, bridges should be built between humanistic therapy and other modalities?
- Are the differences between humanistic schools themselves still significant and worth preserving?
- What could be improved in humanistic therapy on a clinical level?
- What could be improved in humanistic therapy on a theoretical level?
- What does the future seem likely to bring?

I will amplify each of these in turn.

Is the autonomous status of humanistic therapy still important?

There is a powerful movement afoot towards the increasing integration of the various approaches to psychotherapy and counselling: an ironing out of differences, an emphasis on what we all have in common, a simplification of the field—even, perhaps, ultimately the creation of a generic occupation of psychotherapy and/or counselling where different modalities play only a minor role, perhaps being understood as technical specialisations rather than philosophies of therapy. Where do the humanistic therapies stand in this picture?

It is important to be clear that—in the UK at least—this movement towards integration is driven more by the convenience of the state than by ecumenicism among practitioners. Civil servants like neat patterns, and in terms of regulating therapy and counselling this means that they would ideally like all practitioners to be doing the same thing, in the same way, demonstrating the same 'competences' (Skills for Health, 2008). The existing situation, with many dozens of schools and approaches all doing *some* of the same things, in *some* of the same ways, but also all diverging from each other in a variety of *different* ways, is a bureaucrat's nightmare.

The humanistic therapies are an obvious potential victim of the pressure towards simplification, since they have paid perhaps the least attention of any therapy modalities to clarifying and defining their unique position(s) in terms recognisable to civil servants. And this fact is arguably *in itself* a reason to defend the independence of humanistic work from other forms of therapy and counselling. Humanistic therapy is, among other things, a terrain where freedom is recognised as an inherent value. 'Each person's experience has its own truth and it is more liberating and comprehensible to value that … . The only truth is the mind of the seer' (Whitton, 2003, p. 44). This is a powerful position and one worth defending; but it is also a vulnerable one in the current context of positivist hegemony. The state does not want to hear about the inherent truth value of each person's experience, it wants to hear about how they can be got back to work with their symptoms alleviated.

It is rarely possible to make absolute distinctions and oppositions in the world of therapy and counselling; but here are some pretty strong ones. Unlike most CBT and all medical model therapies, humanistic practice is oriented towards growth not cure. Unlike most psychodynamic therapies, humanistic practice is *actively* relational and egalitarian. These two distinctions, as outlined in more detail in previous chapters, are key to the unique identity of humanistic therapy. If humanistic work was to be subsumed into a generic version of therapeutic practice, this is what would be lost.

It is helpful to be clear that the existence of different modalities and approaches benefits not only the client, but also the practitioner (and this is of course also therefore good for their clients, who benefit from having happy practitioners). Certainly, different clients need different approaches which best suit their problems, life situation and personality. But if this was the only issue, one might think in terms of training generic practitioners capable of varying their technique to suit the individual client. To some extent this is indeed a part of good practice; but it is also important for practitioners to work in a style which suits *their* personality, and hence enables them to give their best. If all the psychoanalysts were asked to do CBT, all the CBTers to do humanistic therapy, and all the humanists to do psychoanalysis, then even after retraining it is unlikely that either the practitioners or their clients would be satisfied with the result!

What, if any, bridges should be built between humanistic therapy and other modalities?

Having said all this, there is still an authentic need to strengthen the interconnections between modalities, and for each to learn from the others so as to improve overall practice, while still recognising and preserving the real differences of approach. The humanistic therapies have plenty to learn and plenty to teach. What they have to learn is perhaps primarily about containment and restraint; while what they have to teach is perhaps primarily about spontaneity, mutuality and trust.

The last sentence may have raised hackles on all sides; and it may be worth re-emphasising that we are necessarily dealing in generalisations, and certainly not describing best practice in either the humanistic therapies, the psychodynamic therapies, or the varieties of CBT. The finest practitioners in each modality have already incorporated all or much of what they need from the other modalities. However, the average practitioner in each modality is often very ignorant of what is going on elsewhere, and not equipped to invent for themselves what is missing or under-emphasised in their own training. There are exceptions on all sides, but I am willing to stick my neck out and say that many humanistic practitioners need to learn more restraint, while many psychodynamic and behavioural practitioners need to achieve more spontaneity and mutuality.

To begin with the latter: I suggest that centrally it is about trusting the client. One can sometimes feel with psychodynamic practitioners—especially psychodynamic counsellors, which may reveal a training problem—that they don't *like* their clients, and are constantly on the lookout for attempts to mislead and mistreat the therapist. In a parallel way, behavioural therapists often treat the client as a *patient*, a specimen of pathology, and at worst can act as if the personality of the other person is significant only insofar as it helps or hinders their conformity to the task. Humanistic therapy offers a style which is rooted in an appreciation of human beings and their innate tendency to heal and grow, a style which fosters the valuing of individual quirks and foibles, a principled willingness to follow where the client leads, and an optimism which is itself conducive to therapeutic success.

The weaknesses which can follow from this attitude, as we have already seen, include impulsiveness, over-involvement with the client, a distrust of theory (especially if it involves 'putting people in boxes'), and a reliance on charisma. This is where humanistic practitioners can usefully learn from the other models, which have evolved effective ways of stepping back from the immediate relationship and from identifying *with*, rather than just identifying, the feelings and reactions it evokes in us. This is one of the things that theory is good for: it encourages us to *think*, to fit the immediate experience into a wider context, to interrogate our first impulse for what it tells us rather than immediately transform it into action.

Of course the humanistic therapies already have the tools for this sort of unpacking work: script theory, for example (Steiner, 1990), or Process Work's concept of 'dreaming up' (Mindell, 1987), or Gestalt's analysis of contact disturbances (Latner, 1992), or the Reichian theory of character (Totton and Jacobs, 2001); but these concepts are not always applied to help the therapist 'cool off' and consider the implications of what they feel. And psychodynamic conceptualisations of relational issues in terms of transference and countertransference have a great deal to offer—as is indicated by the very wide influence of these ideas in many forms of humanistic and integrative work, despite the resistance which I have argued is also present.

The least useful import from other modalities into humanistic therapy, I would argue, is unfortunately the most prevalent one: as discussed in Chapter Three, various pathology and diagnostic systems are increasingly a part of humanistic practitioners' mental furniture. As mentioned in Chapter One, this is largely the result of intense external pressure from both state and commerce: the NHS on the one hand, and insurance companies and their case management offshoots on the other, demand a diagnosis if they are going to underwrite treatment.

This is a perfectly logical stance, given that both NHS and insurance companies exist to address medical problems, and therefore need a medical definition of what is going on in therapy or counselling. Since they, alongside voluntary organisations whose funders have largely adopted the same approach, are the only sources of subsidy for therapy, this demand for a medical definition has largely been accepted, and therapy's heritage of medico-pathological labels has been dusted off. This is of course wholly inappropriate to the humanistic therapies, which have stated over and over again that their central stance is to work with growth rather than cure; but few are now willing to stand against it.

Are the differences between humanistic schools themselves still important and valuable?

Like any beleaguered group, humanistic practitioners have increasingly tended to take a supportive attitude towards each other, huddling together for comfort and protection. This finds expression in the tendency, which I have already mentioned, towards 'integrative' approaches—not only between humanistic and psychodynamic theory, but between different humanistic schools. And integration fits with the overall humanistic ethos; as Eric Whitton says, 'one of the most important aspects of humanistic therapy is that it is inclusive rather than exclusive' (Whitton, 2003, p. 38).

However, humanistic therapy can be compared to the Church of England: if inclusiveness is one of its strengths, woolliness is perhaps one of its weaknesses. A united front between modalities which share many values in common is one thing; but it is very different to act as if they are all the same, or interchangeable. There are significant differences between the humanistic therapies, both philosophically, theoretically and clinically, which I have explored in Chapter One; and these will be experienced by clients primarily as differences of atmosphere.

A typical Rogerian therapist, for example, will be accepting, letting the client set the pace and content of the work; while a typical TA therapist will lay out their stall to a greater or lesser extent at the start of the work, explaining to the client how TA works and how it understands people. A typical Gestalt therapist, if there is any such thing (and one must always remember that in each modality many practitioners are not typical), will work less with content than with style, challenging the client to become aware of their immediate experience and how they process it. All roads probably lead to Rome, but these are three very different directions to start out in! And there are also humanistic therapists, as we have seen, who work primarily with embodiment, or through different forms of creative expression.

What could be improved in humanistic therapy on a clinical level?

My answers to this question have already been indicated in previous chapters; they cluster around issues of relationality and unconscious process. I have suggested that humanistic practitioners tend to overplay the role of consciousness and intention in therapy; and therefore, that only limited aspects of the therapeutic relationship are explored, namely the aspects available to immediate conscious awareness. In order to go further into 'relational depth' (Mearns and Cooper, 2005), a third position needs to be present alongside those of client and therapist: the position of the witness, which is supplied by the external and internal supervisor.

A strength of humanistic therapy is its culture of ongoing clinical supervision. It is regarded as a norm, and insisted upon by many organisations, that practitioners at every level of experience have supervision on their client work. In other words, supervision is regarded not as an aspect of training—though it does have this function at a certain stage of development—but as an integral aspect of practice, a key method for witnessing and thinking about the therapeutic relationship. 'The basic humanistic position is that all therapists need supervision all the time' (Rowan, 1998, p. 192). In my view this is a very valuable principle, and contrasts with the much more ambiguous role of supervision in psychoanalytic work, where 'needing supervision' can be regarded as a sign of clinical immaturity, to be replaced with ad hoc 'consultation'; and also with many employment contexts where line management either competes with or, in some cases, replaces clinical supervision.

However there are far too many humanistic practitioners whose supervision arrangements are questionable. I still come across therapists, for example, whose supervision is part of their personal therapy! And even without going to this extreme of potential collusiveness, there are traditional supervision styles in the humanistic world which seem designed more to protect the therapist's ego than to sharpen and safeguard the therapeutic work. There are now some very sound and useful books on humanistic supervision (Proctor, 2000; Page and Woskett, 2001; Hawkins and Shohet, 2007), and these need to be more widely read and applied.

But what of the *internal* supervisor? This concept was developed by Patrick Casement (1985, 1990) to denote the therapist's capacity for insight (Casement, 1985, p. 30). He sees it as 'more than self-analysis and more than self-supervision', being based in an essentially playful capacity to identify with the client, and indeed with other people whom the client mentions, and to synthesise these points of view along with the therapist's own (ibid, pp. 34ff); so that, for example, if the client talks of being angry with a friend, say, the internal supervisor muses that 'someone is angry with someone' (ibid, p. 38), rather than being drawn into the soap opera plot.

Although I have serious criticisms of how Casement carries out this project in practice (Totton, 2000, pp. 144–5), his theoretical account is exemplary, and feeds into the more recent 'relational turn' in psychoanalysis (Greenberg and Mitchell, 1983; Mitchell and Aron, 1999). This development has been paralleled by work in several other psychotherapy modalities (e.g., Hargarden and Sills, 2002; DeYoung, 2003; Dworkin, 2005; Mearns and Cooper, 2005; Spinelli, 2007). One of the most exciting things about this is that it is bringing together both psychodynamic and humanistic practitioners, including body psychotherapists, who share the perspective that relationship is at the heart both of people's problems and of the solutions to those problems. And the humanistic tradition has a great deal to contribute to relational psychotherapy—it has always placed emphasis on what radical analysts are identifying as the '"now" moment' in therapy, the point where the practitioner has to let go of theory and respond from their own authenticity (Boston Change Process Study Group, 1998, 2003).

Humanistic practitioners, one might say, have always specialised in *leaning forwards*—in offering warm human contact to the client, being interested in and committed to their process and willing to offer themselves to the relationship. The analytic tradition is now recognising the value of this aspect of the work. But in order to make the best use of these strengths, humanistic therapists perhaps need to learn more about *leaning back*, creating an internal space for thinking and fantasising about what is going on with and for the client, in parallel with being part of that process. This does not necessarily involve the sort of interpretation of which Rogerians, in particular, are suspicious. At the most basic, it is a resource for our own authentic relating.

What could be improved in humanistic therapy on a theoretical level?

This internal space of leaning back is, of course, the space of theory itself, where we think *about* the world rather than simply being part of it. I would argue that theory is underdeveloped in humanistic therapy: despite the principle of integrating body, mind, spirit and emotion, mind is too often the poor relation.

There is plenty of what passes for theory; but much of it seems to me to be just verbiage, a windy rehearsal of the obvious and the dubious with little bearing on the nuts and bolts of therapy. This probably has a lot to do with my own cast of mind, and with what I personally recognise or don't recognise as offering some purchase on the complexity of the world rather than simply smoothing it over; but from a theoretical point of view, rather than a clinical one, in my view psychoanalysis wins hands down. Humanistic therapy has Big Ideas in plenty; it also has a lively and powerful clinical practice. What seems in relatively short supply is a method of connecting the two.

Those who teach the various modalities of humanistic therapy may be surprised and offended by this statement; but I suggest that if they too lean back rather than forward, they may see some truth in what I am saying. In Transactional Analysis, in particular, there *is* no philosophical overview: all of the many, often elaborate concepts are essentially operational in nature, ways of *describing* rather than *explaining* what happens. As Steward and Joines say quite explicitly, 'an ego-state is not a thing. Instead it is a name, which we use to describe a set of phenomena' (Stewart and Joines, 1987, p. 18).

But much the same could be said of any noun—'tree' or 'mountain', say; and this does not remove the responsibility to make coherent sense of the names we use and their relationship with other names. Without theories of internalisation and projection, for example, ego-states (Parent, Adult and Child) are mysterious and inexplicable. If we look more closely at the ego-states, moreover, we can see, as discussed in Chapter Three, that they contain imported and unexamined theories of human nature and development. TA places too high a priority on being easy to understand (Stewart and Joines, 1987, p. 8): some realities (quantum mechanics, for instance, or human consciousness) are inherently *not* easy to understand!

Gestalt Therapy is an arguably more sophisticated therapeutic system which does indeed rest on a set of philosophical positions. In fact, there are perhaps rather too many of them. Perls identified phenomenology and (a little surprisingly) behaviourism as the key philosophies behind his work; existentialism, field theory, and of course gestalt psychology are also often mentioned, while the trace of psychoanalytic ideas is everywhere present but scarcely ever referred to. Certainly every new theory is rooted in a whole set of previous ones; but when a theory is an integral whole, those roots only become visible when excavated by historians of thought. I suggest that Gestalt has perhaps still to achieve a maturity where its emphasis on here-and-now awareness can articulate fully with its intellectual position. Instead, it trails a bag of theories behind it—a bag which may even be the unintegrated shadow of its insistence on immediate experience.

Rogerian theory is profoundly simple, so much so that it may seem surprising that so many books have been written about it. The heart of it can be—and has been—written on one side of a sheet of paper: the 'six conditions for therapeutic change', or even more so the three 'core conditions', are very brief, but their unpacking takes a lifetime. As Pete Sanders puts it, the conditions for therapeutic change are 'attitudes not skills' (Sanders, 2006, p. 9)—what Amy Mindell (2003) calls 'metaskills', which are in some ways close to what we used to call 'virtues'. So there is a certain incongruity in the elaborate theoretical structures which have been built on this foundation; at its best, Rogerian work is the Quakerism of psychotherapy, concerned with presence not theology.

I suspect that if the humanistic therapies are to transcend their theoretical limitations, they will need to take the courageous step of letting go of their inherited language and terms of reference, and reinventing themselves from the ground up. This is a difficult and frightening move for any institution, and especially hard at a moment when humanistic therapies are so much on the defensive back foot.

What does the future seem likely to bring?

I have tried to place the whole of this short book in the context of the current trend, not only in therapy but in Western society as a whole, towards regulation, monitoring and control of all activities. This is generally justified by appealing to two goals: security and effectiveness. People need to be protected, it is argued, from the incompetent and the ill-intentioned; therefore all activities must be conducted in ways which 'expert' opinion believes to be effective and safe, and everyone who carries them out must be trained and tested for competence in following these safe and effective methods.

It would not be appropriate to take a lot of space here to argue with these notions, either in general or as they apply to therapy and counselling (for such arguments, see Mowbray, 1995; House and Totton, 1997; Postle, 2007). But the point is rapidly coming when the UK government will attempt to impose regulation through the Health Professions Council on psychotherapists and counsellors; and it is already apparent that this will have a particular impact on the humanistic therapies. As I have already suggested, the humanistic therapies cannot easily present themselves in such a way as to meet the requirements of civil servants doing their honest best to establish criteria of effectiveness and safety. As the name 'Health Professions Council' clearly indicates, the psychological therapies are going to be regulated as if they were a form of medical practice. Very few modalities can be easily fitted into this model; but humanistic modalities least of all.

The UK state's involvement in steering the future of psychotherapy is not restricted to the prospect of state registration. It has also committed itself to a major investment in training and deploying practitioners in the public sector. However—in line with the ideology of expertise and 'evidence based practice'—it has been persuaded to privilege Cognitive Behavioural Therapy over both psychodynamic and humanistic approaches.

The humanistic therapies may be handicapped in their principled opposition to all this by twin Achilles' heels: one the one hand their hunger for recognition, and on the other their desire to be of use. Currently (in mid-2008), energy which might otherwise have gone into opposing state registration is being used to campaign for continuing official recognition of humanistic therapy within the National Health Service; and a whole range of humanistic training organisations are hurriedly organising bolt-on courses in CBT. All of this can only have the effect of diluting and disguising the real nature of humanistic therapy, which, as the title of one of Rogers' core works indicates clearly, is to do with *'therapeutic personality change'* (Rogers, 1957)—with transformative movement in the whole structure of the human being, rather than the alleviation of specific symptoms.

As so often, then, we can talk of two futures: the more likely but darker, and the less likely but desirable. The darker future for the humanistic therapies involves an increasing conformity to the social mainstream, and the loss of much of what makes humanistic work valuable, so that these modalities eventually continue only as shells. The desirable future, I suggest, is one in which humanistic practitioners and their organisations reassert and defend the principles on which their tradition is based, principles of recognition for the client's inherent tendency to grow, of respect for the client's inherent intelligence and autonomy, and of integration of the different aspects of being human. At least for the time being, these are minority values; but the minority can often exercise a crucial influence on the mainstream.

Conclusion

It is not uncommon to have problems with those one loves; and this goes for belief systems and institutions as well as for people. This is certainly the way I feel about humanistic therapy: I value and respect it enormously, could scarcely imagine living without it—and yet I can feel deeply frustrated and fed up with it. At times I can experience it as woolly-headed, sanctimonious, impetuous, charismatic and irresponsible.

On the other hand, it is also not uncommon to love those one has problems with; and there is a lot to love about humanistic therapy. For example, its frequent willingness not to know what is going on, not to understand but simply to follow and trust the flow of action and interaction, is enormously creative, and could usefully be taken up by other practitioners. Likewise its openness to the possibility that the client may know best, or that even if they don't, it is therapeutically right to respect their decision; and its perception of mind, body and spirit as facets of a single whole.

But humanistic therapy is of course not a monolithic enterprise—any more than psychoanalysis, or even CBT. There are many different plants growing in the rainforest of therapy and counselling; and although grouping them according to these three large categories is in many ways helpful, it is not even the only possible way to group them, let alone a fact of nature. There are psychoanalysts who proceed in a recognisably humanistic way (Peter Lomas is an excellent example), and humanistic therapists who closely resemble both analysts and CBT practitioners.

I believe that it is crucially important to maintain the current situation of diversity and pluralism in the field of therapy, rather than collapsing all the different modalities into a generic mush. It is possible to combine alliance and mutual respect with the recognition of difference; and this will best serve both clients and practitioners by providing a wide range of choices about how to practice and what approach to seek out. This means keeping firm distinctions between humanistic and other modalities, and also between the various humanistic modalities; while also exploring and developing connections of all kinds between all these modalities, and supporting various forms of integration—but *as new forms of work*, rather than as ways of transcending difference.

Ultimately, the central problem with humanistic therapy is inseparable from its central strength: its dependence on authenticity and love as the essential means for transforming people. There is a profound truth in this, which was after all recognised by Freud: 'The cure is effected by love' (1991 [1906], p. 50). But on an unconscious level, love cannot be separated from hate—either in the practitioner or in the client; and it is only by exploring every aspect of negative as well as positive feelings, self-delusion as well as authenticity, that therapy will lead to genuine freedom. Humanistic therapy can feed its own fantasies of total positivity, total cure, by claiming that everything is available to conscious intention.

Like everything we love—like everything that exists—humanistic psychology is imperfect. Perhaps we can live with that.

REFERENCES

Aanstoos, C.M. (2003). The Relevance of Humanistic Psychology. *Journal of Humanistic Psychology*; 43: 121–32.

American Psychiatric Association (1994). *Diagnostic and Statistical Manual of Mental Disorders. 4th Edition.* Washington, DC: American Psychiatric Association.

Anderson, F.S., Ed. (2008). *Bodies In Treatment: The Unspoken Dimension.* New York: The Analytic Press.

Berne, E. (1966). *Principles of Group Treatment.* New York: Grove Press.

Berne, E. (1968). *Games People Play: The Psychology of Human Relationships.* Harmondsworth: Penguin.

Bernstein, P., ed. (1979). *Eight Theoretical Approaches in Dance-Movement Therapy.* Dubuque: Kendall Hunt.

Bollas, C. (2007). *The Freudian Moment.* London: Karnac.

Boston Change Process Study Group (1998). Non-interpretive mechanisms in psychoanalytic therapy: The 'something more' than interpretation. *International Journal of Psychoanalysis*; 79: 903–21.

Boston Change Process Study Group (2003). Explicating the implicit: The interactive microprocess in the analytic situation. *International Journal of Psychoanalysis*; 83: 1051–62.

Bower, D. and Bozarth, J.D. (1988). Features of client-centered/person-centered therapists. *Abstracts of Papers Presented at the International Conference on Client-Centered and Experiential Therapy*. Belgium: Leuven.

Bozarth, J. (1998). *Person-Centred Therapy: A Revolutionary Paradigm*. Ross-on-Wye: PCCS Books.

Bradshaw, J. (1988). *Healing the Shame That Binds You*. Deerfield Beach, Florida: Health Communications.

Brantley, J. (2007). *Calming Your Anxious Mind: How Mindfulness and Compassion Can Free You from Anxiety, Fear, and Panic*. New Harbinger.

Bugental, J.F.T. (1965). First Invitational Conference on Humanistic Psychology: Introduction. *Journal of Humanistic Psychology;* 5(2): 179–81.

Bunt, L. and Hoskyns, S., Eds. (2002). *The Handbook of Music Therapy*. London: Brunner-Routledge.

Cain, D.J., ed. (2001). *Humanistic Psychotherapies: Handbook of Research and Practice*. Washington, DC: American Psychological Association.

Cain, D.J. (2003). Advancing humanistic psychology and psychotherapy: Some challenges and proposed solutions. *Journal of Humanistic Psychology*; 43: 10–41.

Carkhuff, R.R. (1969). *Helping and Human Relations, Vol 1*. New York: Holt, Rinehart and Winston.

Casement, P. (1985). *On Learning from the Patient*. London: Routledge.

Casement, P. (1990). Further Learning from the Patient: The Analytic Space and Process. London: Routledge.

Clark, M. (2006). *Understanding the Self-ego Relationship in Clinical Practice: Towards Individuation*. London: Karnac.

Clarkson, P. (1989). *Gestalt Counselling in Action*. London: Sage.

Clinebell, H.J., Jr. (1981). *Contemporary Growth Therapies*. Abingdon Press. Online at http://www.religion-online.org/showbook.asp?title=1939

Dalley, T. and Case, C. (2006). *Handbook of Art Therapy*. London: Routledge.
DeYoung, P. (2003). *Relational Psychotherapy: A Primer.* London: Brunner-Routledge.
Diaz-Laplante, J. (2007). Humanistic psychology and social transformation: Building the path toward a liveable today and a just tomorrow. *Journal of Humanistic Psychology;* 47: 54–72.
Dworkin, M. (2005). *EMDR and the Relational Imperative.* London: Brunner-Routledge.
Freud, S. and Breuer, J. (1955 [1893–5]). *Studies on Hysteria.* Standard Edition of the Complete Psychological Works of Sigmund Freud, Vol II. London: Hogarth Press.
Freud, S. (1917). *A Difficulty in the Path of Psycho-Analysis.* Standard Edition of the Complete Psychological Works of Sigmund Freud, Volume XVII. London: Hogarth Press, pp. 135–44.
Freud, S. and Jung, C.G. (1991). *The Freud/Jung Letters.* Edited by W. McGuire. London: Penguin.
Friedman, H.L. and Macdonald, D.A. (2006). Humanistic testing and assessment. *Journal of Humanistic Psychology;* 46: 510–29.
Geller, L. (1982). The failure of self-actualization theory: A critique of Carl Rogers and Abraham Maslow. *Journal of Humanistic Psychology;* 22: 56–73.
Gelso, C.J. and Carter, J.A. (1985). The relationship in counseling and psychotherapy: components, consequences, and theoretical antecedents. *The Counseling Psychologist;* 13: 155–433.
Giorgi, A. (1970). *Psychology as a Human Science: A Phenomenologically Based Approach.* New York: Harper & Row.
Giorgi, A., Ashworth, P.D. and de Koning, A.J.J., eEs. (1986). *Qualitative Research in Psychology.* Pittsburgh, PA: Duquesne University Press.

Goldstein, K. (1995 [1934]). *The Organism: A Holistic Approach to Biology Derived from Pathological Data in Man*. New York: Zone Books.

Greenberg, E. (2003). Love, admiration, or safety: A system of Gestalt diagnosis of borderline, narcissistic, and schizoid Adaptations that focuses on what is figure for the client. *Gestalt!* 6, 3., online journal. http://www.g-gej.org/6-3/diagnosis.html

Greenberg, J. and Mitchell, S. (1983). *Object Relations in Psychoanalytic Theory*. Cambridge, MA: Harvard University Press.

Grof, S. and Grof, C. (1995). *Spiritual Emergency: When Personal Transformation Becomes a Crisis*. Thorsons.

Hargarden, H. and Sills, C. (2003). *Transactional Analysis: A Relational Perspective*. London: Brunner-Routledge.

Harris, T. (1967). *I'm OK, You're OK*. New York: Grove Press.

Hawkins, P. and Shohet, R. (2007). *Supervision in the Helping Professions*. 3rd edn. Maidenhead: Open University Press.

Hayes, S. (2007). Hello, Darkness. *Therapy Today;* 18, 8: 14–8.

Heckler, R.S. (1984). *The Anatomy of Change: East/West Approaches to Body/Mind Therapy*. Boston: Shambhala.

Heron, J. (1981). Experiential research methodology. In P. Reason and J. Rowan (Eds.) *Human Inquiry: A Sourcebook of New Paradigm Research*. Chichester: Wiley, pp. 156–66.

Heron, J. (1992). *Feeling and Personhood: Psychology in Another Key*. London: Sage.

Heron, J. (1996). *Cooperative Inquiry*. London: Sage.

House, R. and Totton, N. (1997). *Implausible Professions: Arguments for Pluralism and Autonomy in Psychotherapy and Counselling*. Ross-on-Wye: PCCS Books.

Howard, K.I., Moras, K., Brill, P.L., Martinovich, Z. and Lutz, W. (1996). Efficacy, effectiveness, and client progress. *American Psychologist;* 51: 1059–64.

Jacobs, T. (2005). On misreading and misleading patients: Some reflections on communications, miscommunications, and countertransference enactments. In L. Aron and A. Harris (Eds), *Relational Psychoanalysis, Vol 2: Innovation and Expansion*. Hillsdale, NJ: The Analytic Press, pp. 175–201.

Jacoby, R. (1987). *The Repression of Psychoanalysis: Otto Fenichel and the Political Freudians*. Chicago: University of Chicago Press.

Jones, P. (2007). *Drama as Therapy: Theory, Practice and Research*. London: Routledge.

Joseph, S. and Worsley, R. (2005). Psychopathology and the person-centred approach: Building bridges between disciplines. In S. Joseph and R. Worsley (Eds.), *Person-Centred Psychopathology: A Positive Psychology of Mental Health*. Ross-on-Wye: PCCS Books, pp. 1–8.

Karp, M., Holmes, P., Tauvon, K.B. and Sprague, K. (1998). *The Handbook of Psychodrama*. London: Routledge.

Klein, M. (1998). *Love, Guilt and Reparation and Other Works, 1921–1945*. London: Vintage.

Languth, J. (1966). Dr. Berne plays the celebrity game. http://www.ericberne.com/nytimes_DrBerne_celebrity.htm

Latner, J. (1992). The theory of Gestalt therapy. in E.C. Nevis (Ed.), *Gestalt Therapy Perspectives and Applications*. Cleveland: Gestalt Institute of Cleveland Press.

Lazarus, A.A. (2005). Multimodal therapy. In J.C. Norcross and M.R. Goldfried (Eds.), *Handbook of Psychotherapy Integration. 2nd Edn*. New York: Oxford University Press, 105–20.

Litaer, G. (1984). Unconditional positive regard: A controversial base attitude in Client-Centered Therapy. In R. Levant and J. Shlien (Eds.), *Client-Centered Therapy and the Person-Centered Approach: New Directions in Theory, Research and Practice*. New York: Praeger, pp. 41–58.

Lowen, A. (1994). *Bioenergetics: The Revolutionary Therapy That Uses the Language of the Body to Heal the Problems of the Mind*. London: Arkana.

McMullen, T. (1982). A critique of humanistic psychology. *Australian Journal of Psychology*; 34, 2: 221–9.

Mearns, D. (2003). The humanistic agenda: Articulation. *Journal of Humanistic Psychology;* 43: 53–65.

Mearns, D. and Cooper, M. (2005). *Working at Relational Depth in Counselling and Psychotherapy.* London: Sage.

Mearns, D. and Thorne, B. (1999). *Person-Centred Therapy Today: New Frontiers in Theory and Practice. 2nd Edition.* London: Sage.

Mindell, A. (1987). *The Dreambody in Relationships.* London: Routledge and Kegan Paul.

Mindell, A. (1989). *River's Way: The Process Science of the Dreambody.* London: Arkana.

Mindell, A. (1995). *Sitting in the Fire: Large Group Transformation Using Conflict and Diversity.* Portland, OR; Lao Tse Press.

Mindell, A. (2003). *Metaskills: The Spiritual Art of Therapy.* Portland, OR: Lao Tse Press.

Mitchell, S.A. and Aron, L. (1999). *Relational Psychoanalysis: The Emergence of a Tradition.* Hillsdale, NJ: The Analytic Press.

Moss, D. (2001). The roots and genealogy of humanistic psychology. In K.J. Schneider, J.F.T. Bugental and J.F. Pierson (Eds), *The Handbook of Humanistic Psychology: Leading Edges in Theory, Research, and Practice.* London: Sage, 2001, 5–20.

Mowbray, R. (1995). *The Case Against Psychotherapy Registration: A Conservation Issue for the Human Potential Movement.* London: Trans Marginal Press.

Norcross, J.C. (2005). A primer on psychotherapy integration. In J.C. Norcross and M.R. Goldfried (Eds.), *Handbook of psychotherapy integration. 2nd Edn.* New York: Oxford University Press, 3–23.

O'Hara, M. (1989). When I use the term Humanistic Psychology ... *Journal of Humanistic Psychology;* 29: 263–73.

Page, R.C. and Berkow, D.N. (2005). *Unstructured Group Therapy: Creating Contact, Choosing Relationship. Revised Edition.* Ross-on-Wye: PCCS Books.

Page, S. and Wosket, V. (2001). *Supervising the Counsellor: A Cyclical Model. 2nd Edition.* London: Brunner-Routledge.

Parlett, M. (1997). The unified field in practice. *Gestalt Review;* 1, 1: 16–33.
Parlett, M. (2005). Contemporary Gestalt therapy: Field theory. In A. Woldt and S. Toman (Eds.), *Gestalt Therapy: History, Theory and Practice*. Sage Publications, Thousand Oaks.
Perls, F. (1969a). *Ego, Hunger and Aggression*. New York: Vintage.
Perls, F. (1969b). *Gestalt Therapy Verbatim*. Lafayette, CA: Real People Press.
Perls, F., Hefferline, R.F. and Goodman, P. (1973). *Gestalt Therapy: Excitement and Growth in the Human Personality*. Harmondsworth: Penguin Books.
Philippson, P. (2002). Body and character as a field event'. Lecture at the 2002 Gestalt Therapy International Network Mexico summer programme. http://www.123webpages.co.uk/user/index.php?user=mgc&pn=10741
Polster, E. and Polster, M. (1974). *Gestalt Therapy Integrated: Contours of Theory and Practice*. New York: Vintage.
Postle, D. (2007). *Regulating the Psychological Therapies: From Taxonomy to Taxidermy*. Ross-on-Wye: PCCS Books.
Procter, G., Cooper, M. and Sanders, P. (2006). *Politicizing the Person-Centred Approach: An Agenda for Social Change*. Ross-on-Wye: PCCS Books.
Proctor, B. (2000). *Group Supervision: A Guide to Creative Practice*. London: Sage.
Read, J., Mosher, L.R. and Bentall, R.P. (2004). Models of Madness: Psychological, Social and Biological Approaches to Schizophrenia. Hove: Brunner-Routledge.
Reason, P., Ed. (1988). *Human Inquiry: A Sourcebook of New Paradigm Research*. London: Sage.
Reason, P. and Rowan, J., Eds. (1981). *Human Inquiry: A Sourcebook of New Paradigm Research*. Chichester: Wiley.
Reich, W. (1972). *Character Analysis. 3rd Edition*. New York: Farrar, Straus and Giroux.
Reich, W. (1975 [1946]). *The Mass Psychology of Fascism*. Harmondsworth: Penguin.

Reich, W. (1983 [1942]). *The Function of the Orgasm*. London: Souvenir Press.

Riebel, L. (1982). Humanistic psychology: How realistic? *Small Group Research;* 13: 349–71.

Rogers, C.R. (1957). The necessary and sufficient conditions of therapeutic personality change. *Journal of Counseling Psychology;* 21: 95–103.

Rogers, C.R. (1959). A theory of therapy, personality, and interpersonal relationships, as developed in the client-centered framework. In S. Koch (Ed.), *Psychology: A Study of Science, Vol 3: Formulations of the Person and the Social Context*. New York: McGraw-Hill, pp. 184–256.

Rogers, C.R. (1973). *Encounter Groups*. Harmondsworth: Penguin.

Rogers, C.R. (1978). *Carl Rogers on Personal Power: Inner Strength and Its Revolutionary Impact*. London: Constable.

Rogers, C. (1985). Toward a more human science of the person. *Journal of Humanistic Psychology;* 25(4): 7–24.

Rogers, C.R. (1986). A client-centered/person-centered approach to therapy. In I. Kutash and A. Wolfe (Eds.) *Psychotherapists' Casebook*. New York: Jossey-Bass, 197–208.

Rogers, N. (1993). *The Creative Connection: Expressive Arts as Healing*. Palo Alto, CA: Science and Behavior Books.

Rowan, J. (1993). *The Transpersonal in Psychotherapy and Counselling*. London: Routledge.

Rowan, J. (1998). *The Reality Game: Second Edition*. London: Routledge.

Ryan, R.M. (1995). Psychological needs and the facilitation of integrative processes. *Journal of Personality;* 63: 397–427.

Sands, A. (2000). *Falling for Therapy: Psychotherapy from a Client's Point of View*. London: Macmillan.

Sanders, P. (2005). Principles and strategic opposition to the medicalisation of distress and all of its apparatus. In S. Joseph and R. Worsley (Eds.), *Person-Centred Psychopathology: A Positive Psychology of Mental Health*. Ross-on-Wye: PCCS Books, pp. 21–42.

Sanders, P. (2006). *The Person-Centred Counselling Primer*. Ross-on-Wye: PCCS Books.

Schneider, K.J., Bugental, J.F.T. and Pierson, J.F., eds. (2001). *The Handbook of Humanistic Psychology: Leading Edges in Theory, Research, and Practice*. London: Sage.

Schutz, W. (1979). *Profound Simplicity*. London: Turnstone.

Segal, Z.V., Williams, J.M.G. and Teasdale, J.D. (2002). *Mindfulness-Based Cognitive Therapy: A New Approach to Preventing Relapse*. New York: Guilford.

Sharaf, M. (1983). *Fury On Earth: A Biography of Wilhelm Reich*. London: Hutchinson.

Sheldon, K.M. and Kasser, T. (2001). Goals, congruence, and positive well-being: New empirical support for humanistic theories. *Journal of Humanistic Psychology*; 41: 30–50.

Skills for Health (2008). *Psychodynamic/Psychoanalytic National Occupation Standards (Draft Version)*. Online at http://www.skillsforhealth.org.uk/page/competences/competences-in-development/list/psychological-therapies-nos-development-project#

Smith, D.L. (1991). *Hidden Conversations: Introduction to Communicative Psychoanalysis*. London: Routledge.

Soth, M. (2005). Embodied countertransference. In N. Totton (ed.). *New Dimensions in Body Psychotherapy*. Maidenhead: Open University Press, pp. 40–55.

Spinelli, E. (2007). *Practising Existential Psychotherapy: The Relational World*. London: Sage.

Steiner, C. (1981). *The Other Side of Power*. New York: Grove Press. Online at http://www.emotional-literacy.com/osp.htm

Steiner, C. (1990). *Scripts People Live*. New York: Grove Weidenfeld.

Stevens, B. (1977). 'Body work'. In J.O. Stevens (ed), *Gestalt Is*. New York: Bantam Books 1977, 160–91.

Stevens, J.O., ed (1977). *Gestalt Is*. New York: Bantam Books.

Stewart, I. and Joines, V. (1987). *TA Today: A New Introduction to Transactional Analysis*. Nottingham: Lifespace Press.

Stone, H. and Stone, S. (1993). *Embracing Your Inner Critic: Turning Self-Criticism into an Inner Asset*. San Francisco: Harper San Francisco.

Taylor, E. (1999). An intellectual renaissance of humanistic psychology? *Journal of Humanistic Psychology*; 39: 7–25.

Thorne, B. (1991). *Person-Centred Counselling: Therapeutic and Spiritual Dimensions*. London: Whurr.

Thorne, B. (1998). *Person-Centred Counselling and Christian Spirituality*. London: Whurr.

Totton, N. and Edmondson, E. (2009). *Reichian Growth Work: Melting the Blocks to Life and Love*. Ross-on-Wye: PCCS Books.

Totton, N. (1997). Inputs and outcomes: The medical model and professionalisation. In R. House and N. Totton (Eds.), *Implausible Professions: Arguments for Pluralism and Autonomy in Psychotherapy and Counselling*. Ross-on-Wye: PCCS Books; pp. 109–16.

Totton, N. (2000). *Psychotherapy and Politics*. London: Sage.

Totton, N. (2003). *Body Psychotherapy: An Introduction*. Maidenhead: Open University Press.

Totton, N. (2005). Embodied-Relational Therapy. In N. Totton (Ed.), *New Dimensions in Body Psychotherapy*. Maidenhead: Open University Press; 168–81.

Totton, N. (1998). *The Water in the Glass: Body and Mind in Psychoanalysis*. London: Rebus Press.

Totton, N. and Jacobs, M. (2001). *Character and Personality Types*. Buckingham: Open University Press.

Van Sweden, R.C. (1995). *Regression to Dependence: A Second Opportunity for Ego Integration and Developmental Progression*. Northvale, NJ: Jason Aronson.

Vasconcellos Project (n.d.). *Our Point of View—The Politics of Trust*. http://www.politicsoftrust.net/point-of-view.php

Vermeersch, D.A. and Lambert, M.J. (2003). A research agenda for Humanistic Psychotherapy in the 21st century. *Journal of Humanistic Psychology*; 43: 106–20.

Wampold, B.E. (2001). *The Great Psychotherapy Debate: Models, Methods, and Findings*. New York: Lawrence Erlbaum.

Wertz, F.J. (1998). The role of the humanistic movement in the history of psychology. *Journal of Humanistic Psychology*; 38. 1: 42–70. Online at http://g.o.r.i.l.l.a.postle.net/hpvoices/wertz1.htm

Whitton, E. (2003). *Humanistic Approach to Psychotherapy*. London: Whurr.

Wilber, K. (1996a). *The Atman Project: A Transpersonal View of Human Development*. Wheaton, IL: Quest Books.

Wilber, K. (1996b). *Up From Eden: A Transpersonal View of Human Evolution*. Wheaton, IL: Quest Books.

Wyckoff, H., ed. (1976). *Love, Therapy and Politics: Issues in Radical Therapy – The First Year*. New York: Grove Press.

Yontef, G. (1975). A review of the practice of Gestalt therapy. In Stephenson, F.D. (Ed.), *Gestalt Therapy Primer*. Springfield, Illinois: C. Thomas.